*

women of principle

*

Women of Principle

✻

Female Networking in Contemporary Mormon Polygyny

JANET BENNION

New York   Oxford
Oxford University Press
1998

Oxford University Press

Oxford New York
Athens   Auckland   Bangkok   Bogotá   Buenos Aires   Calcutta
Cape Town   Chennai   Dar es Salaam   Delhi   Florence   Hong Kong   Istanbul
Karachi   Kuala Lumpur   Madrid   Melbourne   Mexico City   Mumbai
Nairobi   Paris   São Paulo   Singapore   Taipei   Tokyo   Toronto   Warsaw

and associated companies in
Berlin   Ibadan

Copyright © 1998 by Janet Bennion

Published by Oxford University Press, Inc.
198 Madison Avenue, New York, New York 10016

Oxford is a registered trademark of Oxford University Press

Library of Congress Cataloging-in-Publication Data
Bennion, Janet, 1964–
Women of principle : female networking in contemporary Mormon
polygyny / Janet Bennion.
p.   cm.
Includes bibliographical references and index.
ISBN 0-19-512070-1
1. Mormon women—United States—Case studies.   2. Polygamy—United
States—Case studies.   3. Apostolic United Brethren.   I. Title.
BX8641.B44   1998
306.84'23'088283—dc21   97-30463

1 3 5 7 9 8 6 4 2

Printed in the United States of America
on acid-free paper

Of all men upon the face of the earth, we are the most favoured; we have the fulness of the everlasting Gospel, the keys of revelation and exaltation, the privilege of making our own rules and regulations, and are not opposed by anybody. No king, prince, potentate, or dominion, has rightful authority to crush and oppress us. We breathe the free air, we have the best looking men and handsomest women, and if they envy us our position, well they may, for they are a poor, narrow-minded, pinch-backed race of men, who chain themselves down to the law of monogamy, and live all their days under the dominion of one wife.

—George Albert Smith
(1856, *Journal of Discourses* vol. 3)

Prologue

*

I saw this light shining above me in the night. Through it, a young woman of 19 or 20 years walked slowly, dressed all in white. She came toward me and smiled beautifully, saying, "Hello, old friend." We sat in my room, bathed in light, and she held my hand tightly. She had my dark hair, my blue eyes, my full mouth. She told me that I was her only chance—her last chance—to enter this estate [*earthlife*]. She said I must bear one more child, herself, and then my duties would be finished and my name would be written on the Book of the Lamb in the Last Days.

"Please, Mother," she pleaded, tears in her eyes, "I want my chance on earth, too."

She said her name was Gabriela. She kissed my cheek and vanished. When I awoke, my head ached, and I felt chilled all over. How could I have another child? I already bore 13 children. I was 49 years old. Would my body withstand another birth? And what is Jacob, my husband, going to say? He didn't want the last five children that I persuaded him to help me produce. He is never around at this time of year; always in Oregon or Utah on business or with Sandra, his latest wife. It will be difficult to get a verbal meeting with him, much less a sexual one. . . . I know Heavenly Father will send Gabriela to me. I will get Sheila, Jacob's second wife, to convince him to sleep with me. She knows how to push his buttons; besides, she is the daughter of the prophet—he has to do as she says. No man can deny me this special gift-child. I will have her. —Victoria, a polygynist's wife

This book was written in response to the lack of understanding about women in patriarchal religious groups, especially groups that are polygynous, illegal, and renowned for their poor treatment of women. So often, these women are portrayed as oppressed, powerless victims of a male world (Warenski 1980), but as this narrative shows, women are far from being powerless. On the contrary, they wield considerable influence and control over their lives and the lives of their children.

The analysis of female experience in male-dominated religions is highly significant in this day and age. We live in an era when one man can control dozens of women, to the point of convincing them to die on his behalf (for example, the Branch Davidians, ruled by David Koresh of Waco, Texas). We live in a time when a small group of men stand up to the guns of the U.S. government, with hundreds of women standing by their sides (the Singers of Marion, Utah, and the Freemen of Montana). What type of women desires to belong to these kinds of groups? What is their place in society? Who are they? What are their experiences?

To answer these questions, I draw on my fieldwork among the Allred Mormon polygynous group, formerly known as the Apostolic United Brethren. I lived and worked in its northernmost branch in the winter of 1989 with my 18-month-old daughter, Liza. Since that original fieldwork, I have studied women and men in a variety of contexts and many different branches of the same group. Some major findings of this 5-year study of male-female behavior, which was the subject of my dissertation at the University of Utah, are that women are actually *drawn* to the group, voluntarily—and in significant numbers, too—and that men are not the key players in the management of domestic activities and community welfare, as has always been assumed. Women are the key players.

Women did not all agree that they felt powerful in the group. There were various levels of satisfaction and dissatisfaction with their lifestyles. At least a dozen women, for example, said that polygyny was the best thing that ever happened to them, that it saved their souls, and, further, that it gave them something to live for. These women also said that it provided a wonderful environment for raising children and exhalted women to the status of queens and priestesses. At the same time, however, many women, albeit a lesser number, told me that polygyny had ruined their lives, destroyed their self-esteem, and was abusive to their children's health and safety. Many of these women also said that they would leave except that they would lose their children, their homes, their possessions, and their souls.

In spite of this variable appreciation for the polygynous lifestyle, all the women with whom I studied understood the necessity of clinging to each other for survival, being creative in supporting themselves in the absence of their husbands, and manipulating a male doctrine to fit a female reality. Throughout the book, I explore this variability and attempt to make sense of the patterns of female experience described. This book is primarily drawn from my larger analysis of male and female converts, found in my dissertation (Bennion 1996).

For the sake of providing anonymity, I have taken liberties with names by giving aliases. I have also obscured details of personalities and the identifiable events and places associated with them. Because bigamy is a misdemeanor offense in this northern state, punishable by a maximum of 6 months in jail and a $500 fine, it is conceivable that polygynists could be arrested. However, the sheriff of the area has stated on numerous occasions that it is not worth his while to pursue these type of "crimes," and there have been no investigations into polygyny for many years. To insure further anonymity, the individuals in the narratives are cloaked with fictional physical characteristics (I used my own sisters, aunts, and cousins for models), and some of the events in the narratives have been collapsed and telescoped for the sake of brevity and camouflage. Thus, the combination of characteristics could not possibly be linked to any one person. Each name is used for only one person in the narratives and descriptions throughout the book, and the pseudonyms are all popular in the village. These adjustments, however, do not impinge on the reality of events described in the narratives or "composite profiles." What women say about themselves and others, what they think has happened, and how they base their preferences, aversions, and actions amount to a true-to-life picture. It is on this level that the drama of life is observed in these descriptions and accounts of women's lives lived out in the "Principle."

Contents

✳

*

women of principle

*

one

*

Introduction

Women's Place in a Patriarchal World

This book is a study of women who convert to the Apostolic United Brethren (the "Allreds"),[1] a highly rigid, patriarchal Mormon polygynous community in the Intermountain West. The fundamental questions addressed here are (1) Why are women attracted to male-dominated Mormon schism groups? (2) What do they find there once baptized? and (3) Do men and women have different experiences in their progression toward a satisfied, stable life in the group?

This description of polygynous lifestyles extends the scant literature on contemporary Mormon fundamentalism (Altman and Ginat 1996; Bennion 1996; Embry 1987; Van Wagoner 1986; Jankowiak and Allen 1995; Logue 1984), particularly on the role and status of women in North American polygynous societies (Bradley 1990; Cannon [now Bennion] 1990, Bennion 1996). It clarifies the process of female conversion and integration by providing a coherent model of strategies women employ to obtain their ultimate goals. Through analysis of gender-marked conversion and integration in the Allred group, this book also provides relevant comparative ethnographic material for studies on the experiences of fundamentalist women cross-culturally and could be a valuable addition to other seminal studies of patriarchy and female status (Brink 1993; Cannon 1990; Friedl 1993; Sered 1994). Most important, this study of female experience in Mormon polygyny provides one case for the assumption that women are seeking alternative forms of family life in response to socioeconomic hardship in the mainstream.

Research on women in fundamentalist groups indicates that women are drawn to patriarchal movements for more than just a desire for traditional

3

sex roles and male-centered stability. Eiesland suggests that women are attracted to the solidarity, independence, and female forums that accompany many fundamentalist movements (1993:1–3). She writes that although Pentecostal fundamentalist women are triply marginalized—lack of formal leadership positions, subordinating theological tenets, and a subordinating patriarchal structure—these women are converting to Pentecostalism in significant numbers. Women are attracted to this group because of the women's prayer circle, which has given them "a tangible sense of their own capacity to promote change in a circumscribed public sphere" (1993:12). Their involvement in the female association of the prayer circle contrasts with the physical isolation promoted within the workplace. The group is perceived as genuine and unmediated in comparison with the work world, where people put on masks and use technology to communicate.

Friedl (1993:1–4) provides another explanation for female involvement in patriarchal movements. She looks at ideal womanhood in postrevolutionary Iran and finds that, despite the contradictions between the idealized strength of fundamentalist women and their idealized weak, subordinated social position, large numbers of women are attracted to and integrated within the rigidly patriarchal Islamic world. She suggests that it is precisely these contradictions that allow room to maneuver in social and moral space and a variety of lifestyles for women within the matrix of "ideal" feminine traits.

In the study of contemporary Mormon women, there are three feminist theories generated by Mormon scholars and those who are sympathetic to Mormon lifestyle: (1) one that advocates equality, (2) one that advocates difference, and (3) one that emphasizes "republican motherhood" (Hanks 1992:xi). Feminists who believe that sexual difference is irrelevant stress equality and an improved political position for women vis-à-vis men. Those who believe in the "needs, interests and characteristics common to women as a group" stress differences among women that allow a variety of female expressions of power and influence, vis-à-vis other women. The first emphasizes inequality between men and women; the second, variability among women. The third theory is "republican motherhood," an eighteenth-century doctrine adopted by nineteenth-and twentieth-century Mormon women that advocates motherhood as patriotic duty to bear and raise children (Evans 1989:57–58). As feminism encourages housewives to explore the public sphere, republican or compulsory motherhood "redirects women's newfound political consciousness back into the home" (Hanks 1992:xii).[2]

For whatever reason, observers of the Mormon scene tend to overlook the full value of women's subsistence work, their beliefs, their politics, their successful integration, and their impact on society. Furthermore, these scholars tend to overlook the possibility that men are more often those who are discontented and marginalized in these societies. The dynamics of relationships *among* women have also been ignored. Why women are attracted to patriarchal fundamentalism and what they themselves say about their roles in society have not been studied. Because women in Mormon polygynous societies and the children they rear and care for both greatly outnumber men, it seems unjustified that very few studies have yet addressed the supportive power and relative strength of these women (Cannon 1990). Further, few anthropological, sociological, and psychological analyses on contemporary Mormon polygynous family life in general have been conducted (Altman and Ginat 1996; Bennion 1996; Jankowiak and Allen 1995; Singer 1978).

Also overlooked are the large number of groups that have emerged directly out of the Mormon mainstream (Baer 1976:35) that are currently experiencing an influx of converts, affecting the status of Mormon women in a myriad of ways (Bennion 1996). At present, on average, six mainstream Mormon families convert and become baptized into the Allred Mormon polygynous group each month—a fact that sheds light on the growing social and ideological tensions within current Mormonism.[3]

The largest number of converts to the Allred group are women. In a sample of 1,024 converts baptized from 1953 to 1993, 70% (716) were female converts; of that 70%, 20% (142) were blood relatives of other women in the group, approximately 15% (107) were widowed or divorced with children, 54% (385) were single women between the ages of 28 and 45 years; and the last 11% were already married when they entered the group. These facts may help shape information about the attraction women have to fundamentalist groups. Is it out of desperation on the part of lonely single Mormon women who otherwise might not find a mate in the mainstream system? Is it because the prospects for remarriage in Mormonism of divorced or widowed women with children are extremely low (Christensen 1972: 20–34)? Is it perhaps because women find it easier than men to live on "a higher spiritual plane"? These may be some answers to why women *enter* into polygamy, but why do they stay? Furthermore, what happens to the male converts? Do they stay on? What gender-marked dynamics are affecting this flow and flux of converts?

My premise here is that women are drawn to Mormon polygynous groups because they are marginalized in the mainstream church and the larger society. They experience relative economic, social, and emotional deprivation as displaced women in the church and desire something better for themselves. They seek out tight-knit religious and economic solidarity with other women who have the same standards and desires—solidarity that they can find in abundance within Mormon fundamentalism. They want to be connected to, though not dependent on, a man who honors his "priesthoods" and can enable them to bear many children.

Based on 5 years' observation and analysis of convert progression in the Allred group (Cannon 1990, Bennion 1996), I have made the following assumptions:

1. Women are attracted to Mormon polygynous fundamentalism because they experience extreme deprivation in the mainstream, and, in general, women are seeking alternative forms of sex, marriage, and family in response to the decline of the nuclear family and the growing poverty of the mother-child unit.

2. For the most part, women find surprising sources of power and autonomy in the Allred group, although these advantages are laced with certain serious compromises to their ultimate freedom and human rights.

3. Women are much better suited to succeed in fundamentalism than are men; they differ in their motivations and strategies for kingdom building in the system.

These assumptions about women in polygyny are supported by a handful of recent studies suggesting that many individuals in America are turning to alternative forms of marriage and family associated with unconventional religious movements (Altman and Ginat 1996; Fox 1993; Jankowiak and Allen 1995; Kilbride, 1995). The growing number of divorced individuals, single mothers, and unmarried men who live at their parents' residences, gives rise to the search for alternative forms of marriage and family styles. The result is the adoption of polyfidelity, extended-family households, polygyny, and communal housing projects. Many of these individuals join nontraditional religious movements to access these alternative family and marriage forms and to enhance their feelings of acceptance and solidarity with others like them (Bruce 1990:10). Robin Fox suggests (1993:230) that more and more Americans are turning to alternative religious and family movements such as polygyny in response to the growing socioeconomic needs of marginal individuals. Where do single mothers go for financial and social security? Where do lower-class, unemployed men with large families go for social and economic advancement? Nontraditional or alternative religious groups offer marginalized individuals a way to escape the lower status they experience in the larger cultural system (Aberle 1972; Baer 1976:94; Glock 1973:212).

Phillip Kilbride recently generated dialogue on polygyny as a solution to broken families in the United States (1995). He suggests that plural marriage is one remedy for the moral and spiritual chaos in the country, with a divorce rate of 52% and a growing number of children reared without male role models. He discusses, for example, the benefits of plural relationships to address the demographic concerns of too few men for the number of women in African-American communities. Some African-American women are now discussing "man sharing" as a solution for the demographic imbalance.

Many cultures around the world practice polygyny and find it an excellent way to reduce numbers of divorced couples, orphaned children, and marginalized single women. The Allred group contains the same patterns of polygynous relations that are found in Africa, such as the inhouse solution to widowhood found in the levirate and the institution of sororal polygyny to provide for unmarried single women and barrenness. It also incorporates the "senior wife" pattern, where the first wife is wealthier and has more control than the subsequent wives. According to Kilbride, polygyny, as it is practiced in Africa and elsewhere will alter the face of American kinship and family structure for the better. "As a nation, we can't have it both ways—family values and a high divorce rate—without having devastating effects on children," wrote Kilbride (1995).

Kilbride draws attention to polygynous families, such as the renowned Alex Joseph clan of Big Water, Utah, that have enabled the rearing of numerous children, divided the domestic labor, and still allowed the wives relative freedom. One problem I see with his study, however, is his figure (2%) on divorce among fundamentalist groups. This figure in the largest fundamentalist group in 1993 was closer to 35%, based on information given by one of the group's councilman.[4] Although this rate is lower than the rest of society, in a small group, 35% is significantly high. It suggests that, although polygyny may be a viable alternative for many marginalized women from the larger culture, its marriages are not universally stable, as Kilbride suggests. In fact, the nature of marriage and family in many polygynous communities that exist within a monogamous society is extremely complicated and experimental (Altman and Ginat 1996).

Thus, there is in the patriarchal religious movements a grand paradox. In these groups is a dominant male structure that inhibits the free expression of female power, and women are forced to structure their understanding of the world through the model of the dominant group. Yet, in the Allred Mormon fundamentalist group, women have chosen to express themselves with an alternative model, a model that emphasizes autonomy, mobility, female solidarity, and goddess worship.

The method used to gather information about women's experience are many. I conducted the research forming the basis of this thesis in the village anonymously called Harker, at the base of the northern Rocky Mountains and in the suburban headquarters in Salt Lake City, also known as Zion. I relied primarily on three tools in conducting this research: (1) participant-observation and interview, (2) narratives and "composite" histories, and (3) community records.

During the 5 years that I observed the Allred group, I personally witnessed the lifestyles of men and women. Events and conversion stories I did not witness firsthand were recorded through extensive formal and informal interviews of people who knew the subjects well. I also recorded events and behaviors while gossiping with women as we peeled carrots, while shopping at the nearby supermarket, or while sharing testimonies about our mutual love for the Mormon gospel.

During the summer of 1989, I began correspondence with Ben Allred (not his real name), the leader and prophet of the Allred group, headquartered in Zion. He gave me permission to study Harker, tucked up against the eastern slope of the craggy northern Rocky Mountains. There were approximately 900 individuals in Harker at the time of my research. I then met Councilmen Bill Harris (Brother Bill), whose special calling is to establish and sustain the practice of plural marriage among the Harker residents. Brother Bill decided to test my intentions by taking me to what he jokingly called his "leader and boss," his first wife, Shelly, who is one of three female members of the town council and the mother of 13 children. Shelly was bright and confident and seemed to be one of those people capable of determining a person's total character within minutes.[5] She dissolved many of my preconceptions about women's roles in polygynous society. To my great relief, she okayed my request to live with the group and helped to set me up with her sisterwife, Judith. Brother Bill promised to introduce me to other families with whom I could live and work and spent several hours that day discussing the community while we sat in his pickup truck near the town's center.

During this first stint of my fieldwork in Harker, conducted during the freezing months of 1989, I stayed with three different polygynous wives. I learned a great deal from these women about sharing—sharing one's time, one's space, one's material goods, and one's husband. On subsequent visits in the spring of 1990, the summer of 1991, the fall of 1992, and the spring of 1993, I found that much of what is portrayed about contemporary Mormon polygynists in larger society is misconstrued. For one, I was told by many informants that Harker polygynists marry for religious reasons, not material or sexual ones, as assumed. They said that their purpose in entering into the Principle was not to find a more comfortable living style—most live at or below the poverty level in the community—but to find a united pursuit of the Kingdom of God. I saw many men who had previously made good money as monogamists in another area and were now impoverished, unemployed, and struggling to support multiple families, having donated their previous wealth and properties to the priesthood fund. Yet, there were individuals who entered the group and were awarded with additional wives and financial stewardships that increased the financial status they had prior to their conversion. I also observed many people, primarily female converts, who entered the group for the sole reason of finding economic stability and marriage. For most of these women, their expectations about solidarity and satisfaction were met.

Furthermore, many women reported that they did not marry their husbands for good looks or ''sex appeal'' but for their ''priesthood'' and to raise a ''righteous seed'' and that men who entered the ''Work'' for sexual reasons soon left it dissatisfied because of sexual taboos during pregnancy, menstruation, and lactation; disharmony among wives; and criticism from group leaders.

In addition, I found that women were much more visible and vocal in family and community decision making than I originally assumed. Although many women were reticent around their husbands and other men of the community, they were extremely outspoken when with other women, while talking on the telephone, or while gossiping during a work party. Many with whom I spoke, for example, seemed to know what was being said in the male priesthood meeting (the all-male religious weekly conference), even though they were not allowed to attend. (Their attendance is strictly prohibited according to the old tradition of the sacredness of the quorum, which is the number of males required to witness a civil or sacred ordinance.)

In general, I found that the Harker women, though officially subservient to males, *unofficially* complemented the men's authority role with a support system—a system that has worked effectively to provide a haven for women's political, economic, and emotional needs for more than 30 years. In short, the powerful male world of priesthood power, authority, and kingdom building does not exist without the supportive, obedient, and well-coordinated female world (Bradley 1990:16; Cannon 1990:8).

I became aware of the real gender-marked differences and contradictions even before I started crunching numbers. I found certain patterns through face-to-face analyzing, interviewing, observing, and participating in community events. Only later on, when I started reviewing the data on conversion and integration, did the numbers overwhelmingly verify these earlier insights.

Over the course of my research in Harker, I worked closely with approximately 75 women and 35 men, and I was less closely acquainted with many hundreds of others. I attended many community meetings, such as Sunday school, the meeting of the Sacrament, Relief Society, Young Women, and morning community prayer. I did not regularly attend priesthood meetings, which are for men only, yet I was able to get a copy of the written transcripts of these meetings for the last 3 years (1991–94). Although most Allred individuals respected my position as an observer and not a potential convert, a few insisted that my real motives for studying their order were spiritual and that I would in the future baptize into the group, making way for other Mormon intellectual women to do likewise. These proselytizing efforts continued in spite of my repeated explanation that I was not interested in joining the group.

During the second year of research in the Allred group, I began gathering a complete genealogy of 15 extended polygynous families from the Zion City and Harker branches. I diagrammed the overlapping links of individuals in several sets of networks (Cannon 1990) to illustrate the nature of relationships of men and women and the role of women in the family and community. I also read all the in-house literature available (Allred 1984; Bronson 1982; Scott 1989; Watson 1986). After the first month of participant-observation of Allredite lifeways, which was written into a general ethnography (Cannon 1990), I began conducting a series of in-depth formal interviews on particular topics, ranging from living arrangements and ideology to covenant making and marital rites. Finally, I conducted a series of interviews with a handful of women who had recently left the Allred group to understand why some women found their experiences unsavory. Throughout the 5 years of research among the Allred people, I gathered composite profiles, or "life stories" about female experiences in the Principle. I also gathered stories of male conversion experiences told in the setting of the "family home evening" within the homes of the informants. Other composite profiles were mostly narrated informally, while sitting in church together (whispering in the pews) or while visiting the school and watching our children play together. Rarely were life stories about women told to me while in the presence of men; however, on many occasions, men's stories were told to me in the presence of their wives.

In addition to the social meeting hall, I gathered information on the exchanges between individuals at the post office, the community mercantile, the cabinet motor room, the school office, and various kitchens in first wives' homes. Individuals were asked to recount the conditions of their socioeconomic status prior to conversion, factors that influenced their decision to join, and their socioeconomic status at the time of the interview. Implicit in these inquiries were the respondents' perspectives of satisfaction with and integration into the group.

I use the narratives of women's experiences and beliefs as a primary tool in illustrating the kingdom-building process. Within these narratives are patterns that reflect the differences between male and female experiences and the differing strategies of men and women in utilizing the social, economic, and "spiritual" resources available. The narratives in this study are an amalgamation of various aspects of 75 female conversion-integration cases that are prototypic of women's experiences.[6] This method of compression is useful for a couple of reasons. First, it provides further anonymity for those involved in the composite profiles, and, second, it allows me to present the typical experiences in the group in a simpler, clearer format. Third, the conversion stories I present here are situational material that is aimed not at broadcasting individual's idiosyncrasies but at illuminating certain regularities of social processes vital to the community at large. I must qualify this technique, however. All reading is misreading of a sort, so that my selection of the narratives distorts the accuracy of the overall image. Yet, I argue that this selection successfully portrays the gender-marked differences in integration, a phenomenon that is backed by strong evidence: the actual numbers of converts going into the group and those coming out.

I observed that both sexes use gossip as a form of communication and expression, as a means of allaying the anxieties and conflicts associated with fundamentalist lifestyles. Men, in their stoic position as authoritarians and perfecters of their individual kingdoms, are not allowed much indulgence and friviolity with each other or with their wives. Yet, I am aware of several "gossip centers" in which they congregate at certain times of the week. Women seem to access more of these "gossip centers," most often in their own homes. They communicate through gossip stories during testimony meetings, during informal visiting sessions while canning and quilting, or during long telephone conversations with other women. This communication takes both men and women away from the cares and problems of polygnous life and stimulates them to resolve problems by thinking them through and reaching judgments that many can agree with and act on (Jackson 1982).

To better explore women's experiences in kingdom building, I first provide a brief ethnograhic sketch of the Allred people, focusing on Harker the northern branch of the group. I then trace female trends in six areas of life: religion, economics, courtship and marriage, living arrangements, friendships, and networking. In these six areas, differences in integration are most profoundly affected. In each of these areas, I provide an analysis of the differences between male and female progression in the system and several narratives to illustrate the female experience in polygyny. In the final chapter, I summarize the female advantage in kingdom building and provide a gender-marked model of integration.

two

✳

The People

An Ethnographic Sketch

This chapter provides a historical, ideological, and structural framework for understanding the more specific processes of individual choice and consequence. It shows that men and women differ in their progression toward achieving satisfaction and successful integration in the Allred group. This difference is shaped by an ideology that justifies large numbers of women succeeding in kingdom building versus a few men doing so and a social structure that provides women with swifter and greater access to valued economic and symbolic resources. I believe that men and women progress in the system in stages or phases, much like the phases described by Lofland in his study of conversion and integration (1977). Lofland wrote that individuals who have certain socioeconomic and emotional stressors are driven toward nontraditional religious movements. Taking his study as a guide, I am convinced that certain mainstream Mormons have predisposing characteristics for joining the Allred group, and, when they do, certain structural and ideological elements convince them to stay or promote alienation and discontentment.

The first stage is adapting to the new group. Much the same as a convert would see things, the reader will enter the group here in these pages, and experience, secondhand, what it must be like to leave the mainstream world and enter the religious communal atmosphere of the Allred group. Figure 1 is a flowchart diagram of this conversion process for male and female converts. The rectangle at the top shows the point of exit from the Mormon mainstream. People are then confronted with the first question: Do they have tensions or deprivations in their lives serious enough to desire a change? The diagram shows two sets of diamonds, indicating a

13

Conversion/Commitment
Phase 1

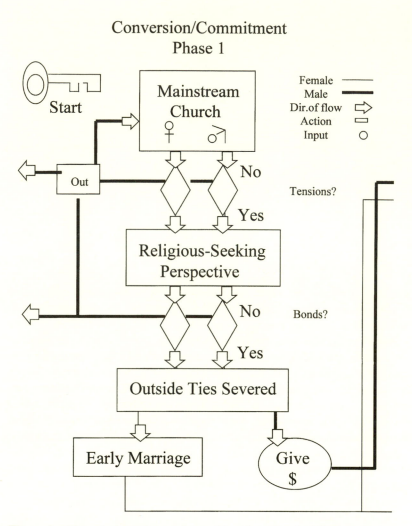

Figure 1. Phase 1 shows how males and females enter the Allred group, having left the mainstream Mormon church. They undergo a series of tests which measure the presence of tensions, new bond formation, and the absence of outside ties. The outcome of these tests results in either moving on toward the next phase, as is the case for most female converts, or exiting the system, as is the case for most male converts.

"yes/no" reaction to which each convert responds, given their specific motivations. Both are predisposed to have a religious-seeking perspective and begin to develop lasting bonds within their new community. Both are expected to cut off outside bonds and make plans to consecrate themselves to the group as an introduction to the next phase of conversion and commitment. Yet, in every case, women have an advantage. Women enter an early marriage as part of their consecratory act, while males are asked to give money, land, or other properties. In short, women are seen to take positions through the channels that are more direct and less difficult, while the men's route contains more obstacles.

Given this glimpse of the options available to male and female converts entering the group, I move on to the broader picture of Allred life that I saw when I lived in the northern branch of the group—one that is observed by many who visit for the first time.

The Women of Harker

Children growing up among the pine trees and scrub oaks at the base of the Bitterroots, 10 miles from the nearest town, know the boundaries of their world. If male, that child must learn to limit his explorations to farming, ranching, and construction work and strive to become responsible and worthy to follow in his father's footsteps. Their lives are defined by strict authority and conditioning for some, neglect and alienation for others. If female, that child must learn to share and become an expert in frugality, submission, and compromise. Their existence is defined in terms of both separation *and* solidarity. Like the fundamentalist women of Short Creek (Bradley 1990:16), where red buttes and dry creek beds mark people's existence, females in Harker are often geographically and socially isolated, living in the rigid "gender-marked world of patriarchy" and established family rule (Bradley 1990:16, Cannon 1990:70–90).

For convert women who are seeking reprieve from deprivations in the mainstream, Harker is the land of promise. It is a place where they can get back to their pioneer roots and live the dream of marriage, family, and community. They know the outside world very well and are willing to give it up for the separated, stark life of the frontierswoman. An interesting point of comparison here is the Lubavitcher, a fundamentalist Jewish group mainly in New York with many secular Jews who have opted for a more conservative religious community and lifestyle and have therefore converted to Hasidism (Kilbride 1990).

From appearances, the single most important task for a woman in this isolated world is to produce and raise offspring for her husband's kingdom. But do they have any other functions? What do women do when not giving birth and caring for children? What is their contribution to community, family economy, ideology, and the social structure? What do they say about the way they live their lives?

In Martha Bradley's study of Short Creek fundamentalists, many polygynist women describe their choices as being restricted and narrow (1990:17). One woman said she realized her limitations when she was 16 and knew that she would "never see the world." Her choices in life at that point could be listed as finishing high school and then getting married, getting married as a teen, or leaving the town altogether and suffer the consequence of family disgrace and eternal damnation. This account of women's choices can also be found in Harker, except that Harker women seem to enjoy more agency in the choice of spouses and have more influence and direction over their household budgets (Bradley 1990; Cannon 1990; Driggs 1990; Jankowiak and Allen 1995). Harker women have a fourth option, which allows unmarried women to leave one branch and join a larger, less constricted branch, such as the Salt Lake City community. I know of a handful of college-bound girls who are attending Salt Lake City Community College and Latter-Day Saints Business College and living with friends, blood kin, and affinal relations to do so.

Another difference is that Harker women have some recourse in their networking relationships with other women. Often women unite with other women to wrestle with their mutual problems stemming from their isolation and, in doing so, make polygynous life bearable—often quite successful, in fact, for some women. Whereas Short Creek men are continuously present in the community, influencing day-to-day activities there, the Harker men are often absent from these same activities and are not directly influential in the domestic decision-making process.

Women's roles and happiness in the Allred group are also influenced by the sheer physical labor required of them to care for their many children and, often, the children of co-wives, as well as the demands of maintaining and managing the household. Women who joined the Harker community in the early 1970s, during the "John Ray Golden Years,"[1] lived in the unfinished basements and attics of others' homes or found shelter in shabby huts and shacks during their first several years of residence. Often, these "temporary" homes had have no plumbing, no electricity, and no central heating. One woman said that she and her children had been "pooping in buckets" and carrying potable water from a pump a mile away for more than 4 years before the priesthood work team installed a plumbing system.

Because of these hard conditions and the prolonged absence of their husbands, who engage in employment in other states or are occupied in "priesthood business," many women have to rely on other women in the community with whom they can share wood, food, blankets, bathrooms, washing machines, and cooking facilities. Harker ideology requires women to have large families so that pregnancy, childbirth, and nursing intensify all the other tasks women normally would have to do. Childbirth, in general, occurs every 1 to 3 years from the time she is married until the end of her childbearing years, in her mid-40s or 50s. Girls and unmarried women (and sometimes boys) of the household often share many of the mothers' chores until their own marriages (Bradley 1990; Cannon 1990).

One major setback for women of both the Short Creek group and the Allred group is that they cannot easily leave the Principle once married or integrated into the group (Bennion 1996, Bradley 1990:18). Because many women have left their former lives, jobs, families, and friends, to join the outcast fundamentalist sect, they cannot return to their former people or find shelter and friendship among them. Their main source of *communitas* and fulfillment lies within the Harker branch. Among native-born women, there is no real job training that would sustain a woman and her children above the costs of childcare, medical insurance, housing, and household expenses. Women who leave the group cannot easily take their children with them because these offspring are considered members of their husband's patrilineal kingdom.[2]

One woman told me that when she tried to "sneak off in the night" with her children, her husband and other male leaders of the sect later kidnapped the children and hid them for several years in various households in Harker. She was never able to see them again. Other women who have tried to leave faced threats of eternal damnation, destitution, and the "darkening" of skin that comes from apostasy.

In sum, though such a system is not necessarily exploitive of women— on the contrary, many find it quite satisfying and desirable—it can be demanding and miserable for many. To better understand this variability in experience, knowledge of the history of Mormonism, fundamentalism, and the Allred Group itself is important.

The History

Polygyny was but a part of an early grandiose scheme of salvation initiated by Mormon founder Joseph Smith and much elaborated by Brigham Young and John Taylor, his successors. These leaders, according to sociologist Kimball Young (1954:29), had been caught up in the American dream of perpetual social progress and believed in a unique theology made up of an eternal monopoly of resources (including women) by males and "whole congeries of gods."[3]

In 1820, Joseph Smith described a vision he had in a grove of trees of God and Christ together. They told him that Christ's church was not on the earth but that he would be instrumental in restoring it.

In May 1829, John the Baptist ordained Joseph Smith and Oliver Cowdery into the Aaronic priesthood, and later that summer the Apostles Peter, James, and John restored the Melchizedek priesthood. In 1830, Smith organized a religion based on his numerous visions and on his translation of *The Book of Mormon*, a record engraved on golden plates of a people who inhabited the Americas before the time of Christ. In 1831, Smith announced the Law of Consecration and Stewardship, a covenant that advised members to donate all their belongings to the Lord, through their bishop or stake president. This consecration of all goods eventually became known as the United Order, a redistribution system that served to unify "a people fragmented by their individualistic search for economic well-being" (Arrington 1955:2–3). For a diagram of how the United Order ideally operates, see figure 2.

In general, Smith's church reflected many ideas derived from the New and Old Testaments, and contemporary Protestant movements, such as Baptism, temple worship, the preexistence, covenants and ordinances, washings and anointings, and "priesthoods." Smith's concept of the Kingdom of God was very much like the Israelite theocratic hierarchy, where God was at the head; men, empowered with the holy priesthood, were on the next level; and women and children were at the bottom (Cannon 1990: 50; Cooper 1990:100–132).

According to Smith, polygyny was a natural part of this holy schema. The Mormon God, then, was seen as a married, polygynous being with human features and a progressive spirit, who encouraged his offspring to be gods, too. Polygyny, commonly known to early nineteen-century Mormons as "celestial marriage" or the "new and everlasting covenant," provided yet another proof of obedience to God's laws. In a vision, the Lord told Smith that "all must obey . . . if any man espouse a virgin, and desires to espouse another, and if the first give her consent, and if he espouse the second, and they are virgins, and have vowed to no other man, then is he justified (Doctrine & Covenants 132:3, 61).[4] Smith promised the men that in raising mulitiple extended families—associated with plural marriage and economic cooperation—they would develop the capacities to govern eternal worlds. He promised the women they would acquire those same traits by subjecting themselves to the righteous rules

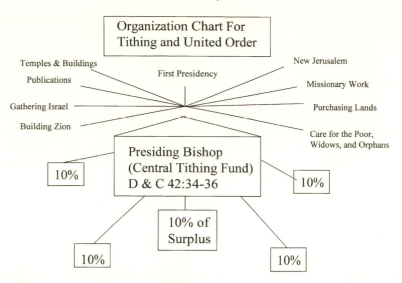

Figure 2. This diagram illustrates the way in which tithes and offerings are donated by individual orders and family units to the central presiding bishop and redistributed back to support welfare, priesthood business, and various other areas of need.

of their husbands. Thus, Smith's eternal schema unfolded into a picture of priesthood keys, holy covenants, and kingdom building.

In 1833, Smith taught his followers about the patriarchal order and covenant relationship of man with God. He referred to stories from the Bible about Abraham, Isaac, and Jacob to provide justification for this kin-based covenant order. The organizational pattern has been summarized by Cooper (1990:106) in four steps: (1) The spirits of human beings are descended from the gods and are thus "biologically" part of a divine hierarchy; (2) prior to mortal existence, humanity was organized into a pattern that included a form of lineage and familial association; (3) in the days of Adam's mortality, a patriarchal order was established that gave Adam everlasting supervision over all his posterity; and (4) this form of patriarchal organization would exist eternally in the celestial kingdom.

Personal relationships within nineteenth-century Mormon polygyny were designed to "inculcate a reverence for godliness, a deference for righteous authority and a preference for spirituality" (Allred 1984:21–28). Ideally, men and women living in this type of spiritual system would be elevated above the cares of mortality—above the needs for clothing, food, and shelter—and be planted firmly on the way to fulfilling the ultimate injunction of Christ, who commanded his followers to "be therefore perfect, even as your Father in heaven is perfect" (Matthew 5:48, 3 Nephi 12:48). Yet, in spite of these admonitions, early Mormon polygyny was practiced by a very small number of elite members of the hierarchy and never embraced as a common form of marriage (Quinn 1985:15), although it did help expand the early church with offspring of these elite members. In general, polygyny was tied to status and leadership and to economic credibility.[5] The consecration of goods to the Lord was met with many obstacles in Illinois, Missouri, and, eventually, Utah. Mormon fundamentalists, as modern Mormon polygynists are called, model their behavioral codes after the early Joseph Smith model of consecration and covenant, priesthood, and plural marriage.[6]

Because of public protests and the accompanying governmental pressures against polygyny, the Latter-Day Saints (LDS) Church issued a 1890 ban against contracting new plural marriages, called the Manifesto (Van Wagoner 1986:iii). Church-approved polygyny continued on a covert basis until 1904, when LDS President Joseph F. Smith, under pressure from the U.S. Congress, authorized excommunication of all who "continued to perpetuate this practice" (Quinn 1985:9–105).

At present, plural marriage is prohibited and relating to "apostasy" by the mainstream LDS Church; in fact, there is no group that is more anti-polygynous than Utah Mormons (Van Wagoner 1986:iii–vi). For this reason, contemporary Mormon polygynists continue to suffer differential treatment and humiliation by their fellow Utahns, a social form of "circumscription" that, I argue, provides fundamentalists with internal cohesion and solidarity. Ironically, many mainstream Mormons still believe plural marriage to be a law of the highest degree of heaven, simply in suspension until the millennium. This belief further complicates the ambivalence that some mainstream Mormons feel toward polygyny and might also account for the large numbers of LDS members who convert to fundamentalism.

Thus, despite the overwhelming similarities between Mormon fundamentalist and mainstream Mormon theology and praxis, members of most Mormon fundamentalist groups vehemently deny that their organization is a Mormon "offshoot"; rather, they maintain that they have been the conduits of the true Joseph Smith gospel—doctrines from which they have never deviated. They generally believe that Mormon Church leaders have lost the major keys and offices of the priesthood and access to divine revelation (Wright 1963:75). They metaphorically speak of the Mormon Church as the mother who has provided the saints with the milk needed to grow and learn in the gospel. The father is the true priesthood found only in the Allred group, which provides the meat of the gospel necessary for further progress in the kingdom. They further state that some Mormons still hold the priesthood, but for the most part the hierarchy is "out of order" and does not have the authority to perform the vital ordinances required before Christ's return to the earth: celestial marriage, baptism for the dead, "endowment" ceremonies, and second anointings. Illustrating their schism from the Mormon Church yet their unique connection to it, fundamentalists often call their group the "Priesthood," the "Father," the "Meat," and the "Fullness" and refer to the mainstream church as the "Mother," the "Milk," and the "Incomplete."

Mormon fundamentalism is further distinct from the mainstream church through descriptions of the character and nature of God. Mainstream Mormons are torn between two poles: a belief that Jesus is the God and "Father" of this world and a belief that he is the "Brother" who is to help his brothers and sisters find their way back to the Father. Fundamentalists believe that Christ is the Son who will take over the Father's place in the hierarchical schema and that Adam is the Father, the God of this world. A further strong distinction between mainstream and fundamentalist Mormonism is the fundamentalist abhorrence of African Americans and other dark-skinned individuals—people whom mainstream Mormons welcome as members. Fundamentalists also disapprove of the way the mainstream church has trimmed the official temple garment to accommodate new clothing styles and altered the original temple ceremony. Fundamentalists still retain the long-legged, long-sleeved, original style of garment and practice the original temple ceremony in their own "endowment houses."

A handful of LDS members who were dissatisfied with the church's abandonment of this "most holy principle" organized an underground order that continued the consecration of goods, the practice of plural marriage, and the original teachings of the Prophet Joseph Smith. This underground movement grew from a dozen members in the 1920s to numbers exceeding 30,000 individuals in 1986 (Van Wagoner 1986:iii). This number in 1994 was estimated to be closer to 50,000 people (Bennion 1996).

The Allred group is one of a handful of fundamentalist groups to have sprung from the original group of underground polygynists. It was formed under the priesthood leadership of Rulon C. Allred (deceased), who traced his leadership back to the orginal movement founded by Loren C. Woolley, who operated under the covert direction of Mormon President John Taylor. Fundamentalists believe that Woolley was present in 1886, when Taylor had a vision in which Christ commanded him to continue practicing polygyny. Woolley, along with a group of individuals who called themselves the Council of Friends of God, led a group of excommunicated followers who believed in plural marriage. Woolley ordained Leslie Broadbent, John Y. Barlow, Joseph Musser, and Charles Zitting to be "High Priest-Apostles" of the Council of Friends. When Broadbent passed away in 1935, Barlow was took his place as the oldest member. Later, Barlow became the spiritual leader.

To find refuge from prosecution for the practice of plural marriage, the Woolley group founded a southern haven in Short Creek, a town on the Arizona-Utah border. Barlow's predecessor as spiritual leader, Joseph Musser, lost interest in Short Creek and handed over the "keys" of the entire sect to Rulon Allred, a naturopath from Salt Lake City. Barlow, however, handed his "keys" to LeRoy Johnson, and to this day the two groups remain separate, though many of their lines of kinship and marriage intertwine. The two groups are the Colorado City group (Short Creek) and the Apostolic United Brethren (the Allreds). The dispute over the rightful heir to the leadership of fundamentalism has spawned a number of other groups, such as the Alex Joseph group, the Kingston group, the Church of the First Born, and the Order of Aaron. The newest, located in Manti, Utah, is headed by visionary Jim Harmsten.

The Allred group has now spread in branches throughout the Intermountain West, totaling approximately 10,000 people.[7] The Allred people are governed by a ten-member Priesthood Council, with the prophet at the head. The group is now incorporated, like the Mormon church, and contains a highly organized priesthood bureaucracy. This bureaucracy is set up to regulate practically everything in a member's life. There is a fine gradation of power as one goes down the echelons from priesthood head (prophet) and council at the top to the lowliest deacon who passes the sacrament on Sunday. The women have a parallel hierarchy, which is clearly below the male hierarchy, in which wives of the leading elite are ranked above wives of the more common priesthood holders. Within families, it is common for husbands to have favorite (primarily, but not necessarily, first) wives, who are ranked above other wives. Children are likewise ranked, according to which of the wives they are born and their ability to bring money into the family (Bennion 1996).

There is a type of ranking within the council itself, which fluctuates depending on the current fission or fusion status of the larger group. At the beginning of my research, Priesthood Head Ben Allred was the highest ranking member, with Brothers Pratt, Widstoe, and Kimball (not their real names) closely associated with this power. Brothers Melvin and Jacob Harris wielded power up in Harker, but in the headquarter branch the

Allreds held power. This split was by no means official, of course, but every member knew it existed. Along with this factionalism was another type of splitting. Each council member was the head of his own godly kingdom; that is, they were metaphorically *and* literally the gods of their family kingdoms. Congregation members who side with one of these kingdoms over another would be "adopted" into them, confer with that particular god, and be called Prattites, Harrisites, Allredites, and Kimballites (Cannon 1990).

At the end of my research, there were several splits occurring. The Allreds were split against the Pratts and the Harrises against both. Because of the excommunication of Brother Pratt for sexual abuse and the death of Brother Widstoe, other members have moved into the forefront, the Harris brothers and Kimball among the most influential. Allred himself, his brother Jack, and his nephew Joe, also on the council, are facing a much weaker position. Because of this, the Harris brothers have an even more powerful monopoly of the Harker branch. In fact, I was told early on that Jacob and his first wife, Louise, are considered the "king and queen of Harker" and that the entire Harker membership is grafted onto this mighty kingdom, a kingdom which is shared with Jacob's brother, Melvin. Those who are not so grafted struggle for political and economic footing in the community. Even more recently, an independent party is suing the Allred leadership for theft and illegal financial dealings, paving the way for Brother Kimball and his followers. Brother Kimball has significant financial holdings in the group and has strong political control over many new families entering the group.

The High Priesthood Council of the Allred group generally authorizes all marriages, grants economic stewardships, approves all policy changes, and calls deviants to the carpet whenever necessary. They hold financial control over dozens of projects and industries under the incorporated heading of Apostolic United Brethren and, like the Mormon church, can do so without taxation on the tithes it receives from members, as it is a religious institution. Some of its holdings include a cattle and alfalfa ranch operation in the West Desert, the X Order, a dairy operation, many real estate holdings, a golf course, and a construction company.[8] The council members and prophet are the corporate board of trustees for these holdings, with each member holding more shares in one project than than they do in another. Members of the group can participate in these projects, depending on their "righteousness" and their links to high-ranking members.

Each baptized member of the group is under the direction of the governing Priesthood Council. All women and children and new male converts and their families fall under the jurisdiction of the branch council of

appointees or, if members of the Salt Lake City branch, the High Priesthood Council. New male converts can, if they obey the norms of traditional society, progress to higher levels of authority in time. By marrying
into an established or "pure blood" dynasty or by being an appointee of
a member of the council, these men can gain prestige. Likewise, women,
by marrying a member of a prominent dynasty and, in some cases, by
having numerous children for him, can gain a measure of formal prestige.

Social Relationships

Like other Mormon contemporary polygynists, members of the Allred
group struggle to cope with many complex challenges: polygynous housing, religious communalism, internal fissions, external political and religious opposition, and, especially, unique family and sect relationships.
Social psychologist Irwin Altman wrote that a central aspect of the coping
process of contemporary polygynists is the management of the unique
conjugal relationships between a husband and a wife while simultaneously
managing a series of conjugal (dyadic) relationships with other wives and
attempting to maintain a harmonious and productive communal life (Altman and Ginat 1996; Cannon 1990).

This struggle to achieve a balance between contradictory patterns of
relations is compounded by the fact that contemporary polygynists rein-
troduced the practice of plural marriage on a large scale only during the
past several decades. The result is that there are few culturally pervasive
and consistent norms and guidelines for living in plural families; further,
there are few standards for dealing with large numbers of converts. Families and individuals in contemporary polygynist culture must explore and
experiment with different lifestyles to suit their individual, dyadic, and
communal needs, and they must struggle to do this in accordance with
their religious principles in the face of economic and political presssures.

A further difficulty in relationships stems from the changing definitions
of rewards and costs in transactions between established, "pure blood"
families, who rule the group, and convert families, who are trying to form
their own patterns of living and bases of influence, based on their experience as church members. Because convert and established families have
differing symbolic conceptions of what the "keys, covenants, and kingdoms" are, conflict is a likely outcome of many interactions at all levels
of society, particularly among wives in a household.

Thus, the challenges embedded in contemporary polygynist relationships are threefold: (1) At the individual level, men must find a place
within the religiopolitical structure, and women must formally submit to

this structure while simultaneously maintaining the productive and reproductive support system that sustains it; (2) at the household or intrafamilial
level, individuals must struggle to form a balance between the conjugal
and communal relationships; and (3) at the community or interfamilial
level, individuals must cope with the differing lifestyles and customs of
the convert and established-family way of life.

The Setting

The Allred group has branches dotted along the Rocky Mountains from
Mexico, through Arizona, New Mexico, Utah, Wyoming, Idaho, and Montana, to Canada.[9] A very small number live in the Netherlands and in
England. A map of the settlements and branches of the Allred group is
shown in figure 3. Though it is difficult to get an exact figure because of
the dynamics of the group, the total number of families in the sect in 1986
was 150. The sect now has more than 250 families. Of the 150 families
in 1986, 139 men had more than one wife. Of that number, 87 (67%) had
two wives, 19 (13%) had three wives, 25 (18%) had four wives, 5 (4%)
had five or six wives, and 3 (2%) had seven or more wives (Watson 1993).
Those members with five or more wives generally held positions on the
council that governed the spiritual and temporal laws of the group, a common finding in many polygynous communities around the world.

Harker (not its real name) is in the northern Rockies. It was organized
in 1961 as a haven for Utah members who were being persecuted by the
law. The prophet then, Rulon Allred, thought that Harker would be an
ideal place to practice the United Order and provide many families the
capacity to live the principle of plural marriage without being arrested, as
he himself had been on several occasions during that time (Scott, 1989).

The town itself is like many other tiny rural American communities,
with a city hall, a grocery, and a cabinet shop (figure 4). The "ranch,"
as they call the town, is run by the same age-sex hierarchy as the larger
group, based on male authority, where women and children obey the male
head of household who holds the priesthood, and the male head, in turn,
obeys the leaders of the community and group.

There are three members of the group's council now living in Harker;
these men oversee financial projects, serve as mediators and remedy agents
in disputes, and sanction all new plural marriages of the branch.[10] Council
members in Harker assign personal callings and "stewardships" to Harker
members and are the only ones who can perform sacred ordinances or
appoint others to do so. They go to and from the Salt Lake branch, where
they also have authority to administer sacred ordinances and duties. They

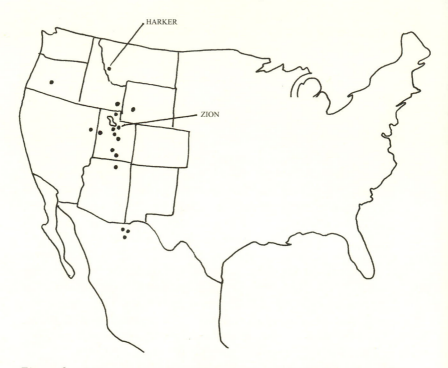

Figure 3.   This map shows the settlement patterns of Allredite orders and branches throughout the Intermountain West. The settlements are established along the Rocky Mountain ridge from Canada, through Montana (where Harker is located), through Utah (where the Zion headquarters branch is located), and down into the Mexican colonies. The Rocky Mountains are sacred to Mormon fundamentalists as the location of "Zion," the chosen land.

also decide who can perform various tasks and reserve the right to ex-communicate deviants. Under the council is a seven-man board, a twelve-man board, and, finally, a general board of all male priesthood holders, which meets once a month to work with civil board and community development decisions such as how to handle the water distribution, what to do about juvenile delinquency, and what to do about funds for new economic projects and enterprises. What the board decides, through the approval of the council, is considered the law, and people moving into the community must give allegiance to this law. A chart of the political hierarchy of the Allred group, as it pertains to Harker leadership, is shown in figure 5.

As in many other Allred branches, Harker families practice a form of religious communalism, the United Order, in which those who bring in more income than others put the "surplus" money into a community fund for roads, schools, or sometimes indiviuals who are having a hard time. Houses, buildings, roads, and waterways are built by volunteers. Most often, however, individuals build their own homes and rely on their own incomes for much of their necessities. In this regard, there is seldom any surplus to be given to the priesthood for its projects.

With so many children growing up in the group, allowing families to

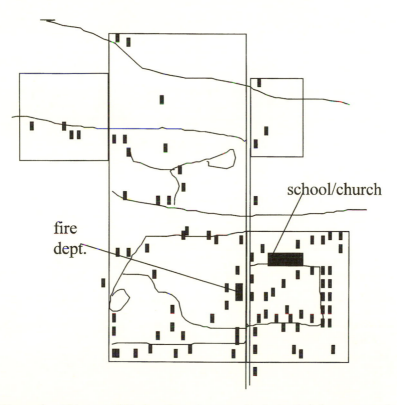

Figure 4.   This map of Harker shows how people cluster their houses around the church/school complex. The town also contains a firehouse, post office, cabinetry shop, and mercantile. Baptisms take place in Sam's Pond, and the trailer court houses many second and third wives. Harker has its own cemetery, cattle pasture, water distribution system, police department, and library. Overall, it is a self-contained community.

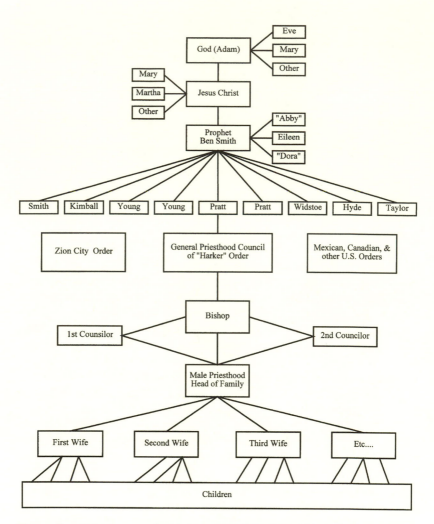

Figure 5. This structure shows the nature of the formal hierarchy in Harker culture, from Adam/God at the apex, to the women and children of the common male priesthood bearer at the base.

keep certain jobs "in the kingdom," community labor itself is a significant resource.[11] Work parties of male and female members of particular branches gather each Saturday to construct houses and buildings, work on the water line or power plant, harvest a crop, pick fruit, or repair fences. However, many families who are on the lower rungs of the political ladder—convert families or nonelite established families—do not often have communal support for needed items. One man said that he needed help with the construction of his third wife's house and finally had to do it himself. One female informant told me that her daughter's baby was hospitalized with heart failure and that the family needed a community fund raising project to pay for expenses. They received no help.

The women generally engage in communal work parties, meeting each Thursday to stitch quilts, sew bedding and clothing, teach children, can fruit, buy bulk foods and goods, and repair and construct general domestic items, such as rugs, storage units, appliances, and some furniture. A sign-up sheet for construction and cleanup projects in many of the group's meeting houses is used to keep extra funds and labor flowing back into the community. The formal structure of male and female projects, however, is not as effective in helping families as the *informal* structure provided by the female network. Even the Relief Society, the women's formal organization, is controlled to some extent by council members and their wives' spy system, and within it cooperative activity is limited to only a few projects a month. The real cooperation, as the narratives illustrate, occurs in the informal friendship circles and household service projects that relay the messages that a sick woman is in need of dinner for her children or that Widow Taylor needs her wood to be chopped. Although many of these tasks are completed with some reluctance, they are, more often than not, completed by women, not by men.[12]

All or most of members' profits and assets must be donated to the sect when they enter the community, which encourages a financial interest in a permanent residence and lessens the chance of members' returning to a former vocation. For example, one member had a thriving fence company and several thousand dollars in gold. Before his arrival in the sect, he sold his company and gave the gold to the Priesthood Council. Another man, on entering the group, lost his position in a successful business when his supervisor found out that he was a polygynist. He now makes far less money at another job and has increased his family with two new wives.

In these two cases, the first member rebuilt his fence company near the group, hired several members, and contributes his surpluses to the community. In the second case, the member and his family are still struggling to make ends meet and often have to rely on the community or on welfare checks from the government.[13] As part of this commitment to the group, one woman told me she had to sign a disclaimer on her children, that required them to stay in the group if she herself decided to leave.[14] To my knowledge, this written consecration form is no longer required and was used only during the "John Ray years." John Ray is no longer a councilman in Harker; he left the group in 1980, when he was charged with promiscuity. However, his influence on members of Harker was tremendous, so much so that even the son of the priesthood head (Rulon Allred's son) was more inclined to obey Ray's word than his own father's word. When Rulon Allred found out about the many unorthodox activities, he was outraged and proceeded to cleanse the branch of this man's influence. Needless to say, many individuals are still living their lives as Ray taught them, and his teachings have filtered down through the membership with lasting significance.

All members of the community, both male and female, have an economic and social stewardship that is their duty and jurisdiction in the United Order. One man's stewardship is the bishop's storehouse, a storage building where dry goods, appliances, and other household goods are stored for those who need them. Another man's calling, the bishop, is to collect the income of all members and extract the surplus to send to the headquarters at Salt Lake. Women have stewardships in the home, as mothers of their children, and often in the community as teachers, nurses, and stewards of specific communal distribution, such as milk, honey, eggs, and herbs. One woman is trained in massage, another is the head of the Montessori program, another woman is the steward over the general store, another, presides over the delivery of babies, and yet another is the *civic* judge of the community.[15] Whereas in the urban community a woman is in charge of the private school system, in the rural area, Harker, this same position belongs to a man. Thus, stewardships change, depending on where an individual lives.

The family, residence, and descent patterns of Harker are very complex and often misrepresented in the cloak of "communalism." For example, because men are so often absent from their various homes, women must form these supporting systems among themselves. A polygynous woman typically spends much of her married life in the same household with at least one sisterwife or with another woman of the community—often a blood-related sister, cousin, mother, or close friend. The male members of these households are not usually permanent residents but are visitors to and from these households. Thus, households are managed and predominantly lived in by the mother and her children as a mother-centered or matrifocal residence.[16] This is not to say, however, that women have absolute control over these properties. The priesthood (council) owns the land and buildings, and the husbands are usually awarded more jurisdiction over them than are wives. Yet, it is the women who manage, maintain, and, to a large extent, inhabit this property.

Large families are prevalent, especially those with two or more wives. Yet, there is great variability in the living arrangements of these families; for example, some families have women living in separate dwellings and meeting all together only once a week, if that often. Others have up to eight wives living under one roof and sharing bathrooms, kitchen, and dining areas, with separate bedrooms for each wife. Some families have the blood relatives—a sister, mother, or brother—of one of the wives in the dwelling. In this regard, families are both nuclear and extended.

The reckoning of descent is complicated, as it represents both earthly and heavenly relationships. Individuals are taught that this earthly life is a blueprint of the hereafter. Because of this teaching, many families trace descent only through the male line; a man's children will remain associated with his patrilineal kingdom for all eternities and symbolically erase their mother's side of their kindred. Some, however, often receive economic support from the wife's side of the family and thus represent a system that parallels most North American communities—namely, bilateral descent. Bilateral descent is a system of recognizing both the mother's and father's kin as relatives, and both sides are utilized for resources and authority. Even still, as one woman explained it, some families trace their descent through their mother's side (matrilineal) to have a stronger position politically and associate themselves with their mother's father's kingdom, rather than their father's (patrilineal). In Harker parlance, "One goes where one can get the best seats in the kingdom," or rather, they trace descent to the line that benefits them more fully on earth and in the hereafter.

The average number of wives per man in Harker is slightly more than three; thus, one wife feeds, beds, and visits with her husband approximately twice a week. In the Salt Lake–Utah Valley congregation, the census is continually changing, but based on the 1986 data obtained from the group historian, the mean number of wives per man was approximately 2.6. This lower percentage is explained by the large number of recent converts from the Mormon church who had not yet obtained plural wives. A small percentage of the leaders of the sect have between five and eight wives, adhering to the sect's codes of building up a "quorum": Three wives are needed for a rudimentary quorum, five wives are adequate for a medium quorum, but seven and sometimes twelve wives are required for the highest quorum of all. (A quorum in this context is the number of women required to add glory to a man's celestial stature.)

Essentially, the wives raise their own children, teach them in the community private school (on a rotation basis with other mother-teachers), and budget their own incomes. (Often one man cannot supply enough food and clothing for three or more wives, so most women work outside either part-time or full time to provide for their families.) Men are admonished to give their wives equal parts of their incomes, after they have tithed (10% of gross) and given any excess profits to the community pot for redistribution. But they do not always do so. The amount of money a man gives back to his wives (after the bishop has taken out the tithe and surplus) varies greatly. Some men have hard-and-fast rules on this return. Others, punish disobedient wives by withholding that month's funds.

The surplus of incomes is determined by the bishop of each branch by requiring a list of expenses from each family. It is recommended by the council that wives subsist on a budget of $1 per day per adult, 75 cents per day per teen, and 50 cents per day per child. This budget is used more by the rural areas, where much of the food is grown and stored and the homes are owned by the community. I was never told, though I asked, what the budget for husbands would be. They are not required to show proof of their spending.

There is relatively little health insurance in the community, so mothers usually rely on home remedies of herbal medicine and massage therapy. Virtually all children are born at home with the aid of the community midwife, and priesthood blessings are conferred on the sick to avoid expensive hospital or clinic health care. There is no central heating in most of the homes, which cuts down on the costs of electric or gas heating systems. Most homes are heated by wood or coal stoves, many of which are fashioned by welding a stove pipe to a steel barrel. One home in which I lived has a thermal heating system in which one large storage tank simultaneously heated the home and the water. Many homes are unfinished and have extremely low or no property taxes.

Harker has its own nursery, Montessori school, kindergarten, grade school program, and optional high school program for members of its congregation. The Harker Academy is run on under $48,000 a year for nearly 550 students, including all labor, supplies, library, film, and instruction materials, all of which come from community and family donations and surplus income.[17] (An elementary school in a nearby town spends $340,000 a year, by comparison.) Women from the branch who have an interest or are trained in teaching, are asked to volunteer their time to educate the children and rotate with others whenever they need maternity leave or a break from teaching. In general, the Harker Academy collects an average of $20 per month per child from nearly every household to operate the school.

In addition to the school, the bishop's storehouse, and various types of in-house industries, such as construction, cabinet making, and midwifery, there are community bazaars held seasonally by the Relief Society, where goods and foods are made and contributed for sale on behalf of those in the community who need emergency funds. These bazaars are internally directed by the female network. There are also fairs, carnivals, and "dime-a-dip" dinners held to pay for medical bills for the ill or help a mother whose husband is out of town and needs financial aid. The children also host talent shows to raise money for youth projects. Several informants suggested that these bazaars and fund-raising projects were strictly to benefit "name" (pure blood) family members and not lower-ranked individuals. I inquired about the last 5 years of projects and was told eight stories of charity drives that benefited sick and ailing individuals. Six of them were members of established, prominent families.

In spite of the advantages of group life—a private school program, effective religious indoctrination and socialization, and religious autonomy from the larger culture—informants admit that the branches are far from the heavenly ideal of the United Order. One of the problems is the failure of the the order to provide a comfortable living for *all* members of the sect. One house in which I visited was in poor condition, with mildew on the walls, insects crawling in the corners, and children wearing outgrown, shabby clothes. Another house in which my daughter and I lived had plush carpet in every room, a highly efficient woodstove with insert, elegant paintings, and Victorian furniture. Some members complained that there is not perfect obedience to the rules of the order or total willingness to share time, money, and labor. The residents of one branch, for example, are encouraged to shop only at the local mercantile, the only community commercial enterprise. Yet, many find much cheaper prices at the larger supermarket in the nearby town. Members are also encouraged to pay a 10% tithe and contribute any surplus to the community funds. Not all members are doing this—and many are becoming more extravagant in their spending and expenses—leaving little "excess" for the communal pot. Often, insurance claims from accidents such as a fire or car wreck are taken by members of the council and not redistributed to the victims, especially if the property destroyed is priesthood-owned.[18] It is this inconsistency in donations, tithes, labor for community projects, priesthood prerogatives, treatment of wives and children, and families' well-being that is a prime cause of conflict between individuals in the Principle (Bennion

1996). I believe that Harker residents cope with this unpredictability in finances and living conditions by relying on the economic and sociological activities of the female network.

In short, much of the United Order's strength lies in the informal networking developed among co-wives that helps families to better manage their finances.[19] The women bargain and barter in the distribution of food items, clothing, baby items, and household goods, and, as a result of this activity, many families are provided for who normally would be forced to go on welfare or leave the community altogether.

For the most part, the sexual division of labor of Harker follows that of other small communities in the intermountain states area, where men work outside the home and women work in the home and care for children. The difference in Harker is that there are far more women than men; more than half the women are wage earners so there are twice as many women workers as men. Because these women often live in the same dwelling or at least in the same village with their co-wives, one is able to care for the another's young children while that woman works and earns income for the larger family. Again, some women may prefer that their co-wives not care for their children, but they have no other source of help and so allow it. Women also often rotate other duties such as cooking, cleaning, and home maintenance. Even those who stay at home tending their own and their co-wives' children are contributors to the labor force of the group.

Men, individually, bring in more dollars (construction workers and auto parts salesmen make more per hour than do secretaries and nurses), but women bring in more money collectively, by sheer force of their numbers. Women's work in the home is difficult to equate to dollars, and it is combined with unorthodox and informal scrounging and penny-pinching. While men's work in the town's shops and garages is considered valuable labor, rather than putterings, women's work in the domestic sphere is not acknowledged formally by the group. In chapter 4, I examine the nature of this domestic work and show through the story of Judith how this type of labor is valuable in its contribution to family and community subsistence. I also show how another woman receives monthly welfare and food stamps that provide for her husband's other wives and, through this activity, although unorthodox and disapproved of, is able to make life for herself and others more bearable.

Courtship and marriage patterns in Harker differ widely from the American norm. The average age at first marriage for "established" women is 17 to 18 and for convert women is 19, though 15 and 16 for both are not unheard of.[20] These data on age at first marriage were taken over the last 20 years from a sample of 55 women, 35 of whom were established. There is some indication that woman marry so young because they have been trained to value marriage and childbirth, and the option for pursuing a job or higher education is not as attractive. Courtship itself is usually short, lasting from a few weeks to 6 months. Marriage decisions, ideally, are considered religious ones, not open to private concerns unless those private concerns parallel priesthood prerogatives. In other words, the council members of Harker *ultimately* exert influence on the distribution of wives, though they may not intentionally or directly do so. I found through many interviews with married women, however, that they were allowed to take matters into their own hands in selecting their husbands without too much objection from the priesthood. And women are encouraged to practice "hypergamy," or marrying up, to be exalted by a man who holds a high spiritual or priesthood rank. Because women are considered, for the most part, more spiritually worthy than men, this is a grand task. The Allredites take the counsel of Brigham Young in his discourse on divorce and marriage (1861), which requires a woman who is released from a marriage union to find a man with "higher priesthoods" than her former husband. Thus, women in this type of system, ideally, gain a better status through marrying the elite of the group, while men marry downward.

Often, there is a signficant discrepancy between the ideal and reality. Some *men* marry into pure blood families and advance their status. Furthermore, women of established families sometimes marry low-ranking convert or established men. The check on marriage choices and the sanctioning of plural wives is up to the council, and in this way they can regulate the advancement and status of both men and women. It is quite common, for example, for the council matchmaker to advise men when and whom to marry and how to live in plural households, whether that counsel is sought or not. I was told that this custom allows the leader of the branch—who knows everyone by name and probably has an idea of how well two people might suit each other and be materially provided for—to approve the right decision for the couple. In one case, for example, there was a "problem girl who had a promiscuous nature" who needed the special attention of the council. The council, her father, and the victim of her promiscuity (a man for whom she babysat) met together to discuss the possibility of a union. The girl was then informed, and in a relatively short time she went from being a part-time baby-sitter and girlfriend to a man's daughter to being his third wife and her friend's "aunt." In cases like these, it is generally agreed that there is no place for tender sentiments or romantic love; on the contrary, relations are based on practical and ideological needs (Young 1954:13). In other cases, the parents make the decisions and suggest them to the council. In most cases, the couple themselves make the choice and then gain the council's approval. These young-couple marriages are getting more common than in John Ray's time, and, as in the early church (Embry 1987), a young man usually marries a woman near his own age for a first wife, although later marriages tend to see increasing gaps in the ages of bride and groom.

The procedure for a polygynist married man in courting a single girl (a common practice in Harker) is to first approach his wives about his decision and gain their approval, although some do not feel this is a necessary step. He then approaches the matchmaker of the town, Councilman Melvin Harris, or, better yet, gains the approval of Priesthood Head Ben Allred himself. In one case, where it was clear the first wife did not like her husband's choice, he went first to the councilman for his approval, got it, and then told his wife. Another common practice is for a man who sees a new woman in the community to have his wife go and make introductions and "scope her out" for him. One woman recalled the time when her husband and his brother both asked their first wives to get acquainted with the same new convert at the same dance. The wife of the brother told her to stay clear, as her husband wanted first dibs on the new woman. The woman said with pride that she was able to court the new woman with greater finesse, and eventually the new woman joined her family.

The procedure of a woman courting a married man, however, is quite different. She either gets friendly with the senior or latest wife, or she subtly flirts with the prospective husband at the community dances or in church. Another method is to point out the prospect to the matchmaker and he then negotiates it. Again, it is ideally up to the woman to make the final decision.

Some women stated that if a woman thinks she can possibly grow to love a man, she tells her father, who tells the matchmaker, who then tells the man.[21] If a man wants to, he may go to the woman's father and ask to court his daughter. After the father speaks to the woman about it, the man then begins courting the daughter. Sometimes, as in the case of a man whose wives did not approve of his choice of brides, he ceased his courtship with her and found a woman whom his wives liked much better. In this way, to a great extent, the senior wife exercises a degree of control over the choice of subsequent wives. Senior wives are in an excellent position to see that their husbands' future mates are both amenable and cooperative. Women sometimes have recommended their sisters, cousins, or best friends as polygynous wives for their husbands and, as a result, helped to preserve domestic tranquility and provided a kind of social security for the less fortunate members of their families.[22] It is quite common

(12 marriages of 35) for first wives to court women who they considered to be less attractive than themselves. I saw a pattern of second and third wives who were overweight, less pretty, and married to their husband by the first wife's "doing," not the husband's.

During courtship, there is also a great deal of variation in the degree of secretiveness maintained and in the opportunity couples have to visit each other. Some couples, usually young ones, are known by everyone to be going together. This kind of union tends to be celebrated more openly. When a married man courts an unmarried women, however, more discretion is used.

In a gathering of women at the 4-Bs restaurant one afternoon in Harker, I asked several woman what they thought men sought in a new mate. One told me that many married men are anxious for a younger bride for child-bearing purposes, yet some want an older one with more maturity and experience to manage the household. Another elderly woman then retorted, "I don't believe that men actually *seek* out mature women. The priesthood orders them to marry them so they will be taken care of. Most older women are 'put out to pasture.' "

Overall, I found that the range of marital prospects in Harker is often wider and richer for girls and unmarried women than for men, as most of the older women are already married, unless recently widowed or divorced, and every man above the age of 18, whether married or not, is eligible for marriage. The divorce rate is approximately 35% out of a marriage pool of 95%, based on the 1992 statistics announced in a priesthood session.[13]

According to Allred doctrine, individuals may be married in three different ways: (1) the secular "time only" marriage, in which the bonds of matrimony end at death; (2) the "time and eternity" marriage, in which the bonds of matrimony last forever; and (3) the "eternity only" marriage, in which those who had spouses who predeceased them without being properly sealed by the priesthood are provided for. This third way quite commonly occurs when a widower or widow who converted to the Work has a dead spouse married to them for eternity to allow them to be reunited in the hereafter. This scheme provides a man with an almost unlimited number of wives in heaven; a woman whose husband died first would be able to be married to another for "time."

Though marriage tends to bind men and women together in celestial union to create a conjugal unit, this unit is overlapped with other conjugal units—sometimes five or six. As a result, a new wife sometimes builds stronger bonds with her sisterwives in day-to-day contact with them than she does with her husband, who is either visiting his other wives or working long hours trying to support his brood. I was told by one woman that because of the ease with which women bond with other women, husbands often find it difficult to become intimate or close in friendship with all their wives. Not only do they spend less time with their wives but also they are often not able to break with the traditional male superiority–female inferiority codes in order to establish simple friendship with their wives. One man who married two sisters found that the sisters got along better together than those wives who were not related; they could draw on similar backgrounds to deal with the pressures of plural living. The practice of marrying sisters and blood kin, as I point out in chapter 5, is not as common as it was 20 or 30 years ago. Most women come together in a marriage because they were both attracted to the same man, they met in college, or they found commonalities in doctrine or socialization practices. Those women who are thrust together in one family and have nothing in common find it very difficult to cooperate, much less love each other for eternity.

One woman said of her co-wife relations, "It is a joy to have a companion with whom I can share sorrow and happiness, sickness and health . . . to have someone to lean upon and turn to for assistance, to know that your children are receiving a mother's loving care" (Musser 1948:26). Another, however, said that she longed for the day when her sisterwife left the town, as she found it unbearable to be around her for more than 5 minutes.

In her 1990 article, Bradley made the analogy of co-wife friendship to the friendship between a husband and wife in a close monogamous marriage. This analogy fits Harker's case. One wife said to her husband, "It's more important that she [a new wife] get along with us than with you. A plural wife doesn't see much of her husband, but she is entering into the family of her sisterwives" (Taylor 1953:78).

The shared persecution, the shared economic hardships, and perhaps, in some cases, the shared physical intimacies during the long absences of their husband increase wives' commitment to each other.

Some women, I found, do not agree that all co-wives get along well; in fact, one informant stated that co-wives are natural rivals and enemies who "resent and despise the fact that their husband is having sex with them, is attracted to them, and is taking better care of their children" than their own. I was frequently told that women go through a period of "hate" for each other when first brought together by their husband. One woman "got so bent out of shape" by the arrival of her new co-wife that she would wander around "listlessly" through the woods, crying and muttering statements about dying. Yet, she and the co-wife are now quite good friends and spend hours talking on the phone. When I asked what changed the woman's mind about her co-wife, she said they share a love for ''perverse'' gossip and enjoy manipulating others' resources. Rather than love, this particular relationship has been described as ''tolerated'' and ''the sisterhood of malice.''

Thus, paradoxically, fundamentalist women often live a ''split'' existence of exalted love and suppressed contempt for their sisterwives. This contradiction is even more complicated in that the patriarchal order stresses a woman's need for male guidance, support, and control—an ideal that is not expressed in the reality of day-to-day living. In day-to-day living, often the very women they wish to avoid are the women with whom they *must* cooperate. The very marginalized limitations that attract and *bind* women to Harker are, ironically, the primary motivating factors behind the success of female solidarity and unity.

Female Experience: The Narrative Voice

The next several chapters are narratives drawn directly from interviews in which I asked women to tell me their life composite histories (''stories'' for short) and why they entered into the Principle. Each chapter illustrates key points about the validity and importance of the female network and includes a brief description of ideology, economy, socialization, courtship, marriage, or kinship, whichever pertains to that particular woman's story. It also describes women who did not get along or had difficulties in resolving conflicts in the polygynous lifestyle.

The first narrative chapter, chapter 3, looks at how ideology affects women's roles in society and their bonds with one another and at how the belief system is not always representative of actual behavior. Specifically, these first stories illustrate womens' attraction to the Work based on their perceptions of divine exaltation and being of ''one flesh'' in the gospel. They show how three women use the powers inherent in their status as priestesses and potential queens to heal the sick, bless their children, and pave a path for their own goddesshood.

Chapter 4 examines narratives dealing with economic challenges related to Mormon polygnous lifestyles, including how one woman engaged in a series of reciprocal exchanges with other women to feed and clothe her five children. Chapter 5 is comprised of three narratives: a 17-year-old woman approaching marriage, a young married second wife, and a middle-aged first wife. All these narratives shed light on the unique features of socialization, courtship, and celestial marriage that are vital in understanding how the female network operates and maintains female solidarity. In chapter 6, I present two stories of co-wives' strategies in their living arrangements and domestic management. The first woman is a second wife who feels she is being crowded out by her co-wife; the second woman feels the opposite and wishes she could live with her scattered co-wives in one communal unit. Chapter 7 deals with sickness, aging, barrenness, and death. It examines the lives of four women who have relied heavily on the female network in order to survive poverty, cancer, unfulfillment, widowhood, childlessness, spinsterhood, loneliness, homelessness, and death. In chapter 8, by way of conclusion, I examine what the narratives tell us about co-wife strategies for survival and happiness in a strict patriarchal society. I also note incidents of conflict, strain, and tension between co-wives' that illustrate how the network does not work for every woman and how some polygynist wives, though a minority, attempt to leave the sect because of abuse, abandonment, estrangement, and alienation. In the conclusion, I discuss the implications that the influx of mainstream Mormon men and women into fundamentalism has on the study of Mormon fundamentalist families and predict that the nature of female involvement in the formal realm of society will, by necessity, be enhanced, as will their formal callings and statuses; otherwise, more and more women will find ways of leaving the group for a more supportive environment. For example, during the last several months, I have been invited to attend female support groups and ''salons,'' where women speak out against fundamentalist culture and form bonds of friendship and *communitas* with others who say they don't mind working with other women: ''It is the men that make polygyny difficult.'' These groups are growing in number and include many first wives, who, now that their children are grown, desire to leave the Allred group.

three

*

Ideological Blueprints

Charters for Female Status and Satisfaction

Women create their own ideological framework in the Allred group. The narratives in this chapter provide examples of how women gain autonomy and empowerment through certain unique religious codes and principles, centered in their own experience. These narratives are presented in a realistic fashion that protects the identities of informants. Throughout these narratives, convert women have an advantage over convert men in gaining access to valued rituals and spiritual powers and in finding justification through scriptures and folklore for their empowerment.

Ideology

Harker formal religion is centered on three main principles of the Joseph Smith gospel: celestial marriage, kingdom building, and the law of consecration (the United Order). Intrinsic in all of these principles is the bedrock of priesthood power—a power that is recognized as being directly from God and that gives a man ultimate control over his wives and children, as well as over "Gentiles." Harker members generally believe that men rule and women and children obey; women are under strict obligations never to say no to their husband's demands. In broader terms, priesthood is seen as the power of God used by both male and female for the perpetuation of a righteous seed. Men receive this privilege by the "laying on of hands" of higher ranking members of the priesthood, just as Christ ordained his disciples 2,000 years ago. Ideally, in the process of ordination, the father is in charge of his own son's progress. In Harker, however, it is the bishop who appoints young men to their priesthood offices.

41

At the age of 12, a boy is ordained to be a deacon, at about 14 he becomes a teacher, and at 16, a priest. These lower ranks are in the Aaronic priesthood. The higher level begins with age 19, when a young man becomes an elder. He then becomes a "seventy," a term used to refer to the number of married men required to make up a quorum, and then he becomes a high priest. These higher ranks are in the Melchizedek priesthood.

Women play little role in this formal priesthood schema. A woman may, if worthy and married to a high-ranking Melchizedek priesthood holder, tap into this power when she is with him. Council members often reprimand women who access this priesthood for their own means, however, and limit the flexible use of priesthood among lower ranking men as well.

In the larger Allred group, there is a belief that a woman who is married and has her endowments ranks higher in the priesthood than younger, unmarried, unendowed men. The priesthood itself does not come into its full power until a man and a woman are joined through the Holy Spirit of Promise or even until they have both received their "second anointings," making them king and queen of their earthly kingdom.

Harker formal ideology suggests that one of the basic responsibilities of a priesthood holder is to ensure that he and his family receive the ordinances for which they are eligible, such as blessings, baptism, and financial stewardships that will support them. Only the man, as a priesthood bearer, can formally perform the ordinances. However, as shown in the composite profiles of Jan, Liz, and Mary in this chapter, women participate in these ordinances on certain levels. One woman in the branch is appointed to bestow sacred "mother's blessings" on the heads of women who have just conceived. Also, other women who are isolated can call upon Jesus to bless their children when needed.

Women, with their husbands, form the holy priesthood union that is represented symbolically by Adam and Eve, often called "the divinely established priesthood," "the fullness," "the Most Holy Principle," and "the new and everlasting covenant." It is rare, however, that women participate publicly in any type of blessing or ordinance, because it is generally frowned on by the council leaders of the branch.

Plural Marriage

Celestial marriage was established with the primary purpose of raising up a plentiful, righteous seed unto the Lord.[1] As James Powell, an ardent follower of the Principle, wrote in his diary (1871): "Celestial marriage is one of the most sacred and essential principles of the gospel, for without it neither we nor our forefathers can claim our wives, nor our wives claim us, and enter upon our exaltation in the eternal worlds."[2]

Polygyny was said to be a divine principle "dedicated by the Gods for the perpetuation of life and birth of earths" (Musser 1944:102). According to Harker worldview, there are three good reasons to enter into plural marriage: (1) Old Testament prophets, such as Abraham, had plural wives; (2) plural marriage gives one access to eternal worlds as a god; and (3) Jesus and God (Adam) both had plural wives (Doctrine & Covenants: 132: 28).[3] Each wife has the same opportunity to be "one flesh" with her husband, as Jesus was "one flesh" with his apostles. No matter how many wives a man has, he and each of his wives will be one (Kraut 1983). When this man-woman bond is formed, it is easier to form bonds between wives. When a family is united in all things, they are prepared to unite themselves with heaven, and all are one with God.[4]

According to one resident, polygyny also serves the purpose of washing away the filth of the "daughters of Zion" by turning them into plural wives, as recorded in Isaiah 4:4. In Harker, it is often suggested that if only polygyny were adopted throughout the United States, all the prostitutes would be eliminated. In short, polygyny became the catch-all solution for prostitution, infidelity, homosexuality, spinsterhood, childlessness, and various types of sexual sin (Bradley 1990). This theme is similar to what was preached in the early church.

The appropriate behavior of husbands and wives is that of ruler and subject, based on the teachings of Joseph Smith (Musser 1944, 1948). Husbands must be instructional and dominating, and wives must be obedient and respectful. Further requirements for women are summarized in Musser's editoral in *Truth* in 1948: "Thy desire shall be to thy husband, and he shall rule over thee." Women are taught to "respect and revere themselves, as holy vessels, destined to sustain and magnify the eternal and sacred relationship of wife and mother." A wife is the "ornament and glory of man; to share with him a never fading crown, and an eternally increasing dominion" (1948:134). Musser also wrote that man "shall fight the physical battles in protection of his loved ones, and bring into the home the necessaries of life." The wife "adorns the home, conserves the larder and renders the habitation an earthly heaven where love, peace, affection, gratitude, and oneness shall abound, she the queen and he the king" (1948: 134).

The Harker ethos does not celebrate sexuality but often treats it with caution as a necessary evil—at best a force which men must learn to control and from which pregnant, lactating, and menstruating women must be protected. But women do not have much trouble limiting their number of children if that is their aim. Sharing a husband with five other women often is a good means of contraception. Another way of avoiding having children is to space conception at least 18 months apart, which conserves the mother's health and enables her to bring forth healthy and beautiful children. Because the single most important role is motherhood, a task associated with celestial rewards and kingdoms of glory, barrenness is seen as a reproach—God's curse on the woman and her husband.

Kings and Kingdoms

The structure of male hierarchy in the patriarchal order is based on "priesthood" powers and authorities and is centered in the prophet and his council. Although these men defer to Jesus Christ and Adam-God, this deference is vaguely interpreted. Every member understands explicitly, however, the power and control of the council, as they direct their behavior in very overt ways. All must strictly obey this male theological structure and dedicate their lives in the service of their "Father in Heaven." Council members themselves become gods to their constituents. Their kingdoms are ranked higher than other men's kingdoms, and it is generally known that all members are adopted or grafted onto the high-ranking dynasty, the Harris family.[5] Figure 6, drawn up by early apostle Orson Pratt, illustrates the design of a man's kingdom. Women are told they will be blessed for their obedience to the council and to their husbands and rewarded with thrones of their own, next to their husband's throne, to rule over heavenly kingdoms and peoples (*Doctrine& Covenants* 132).

Harker saints believe that God is an exalted man and that, if they are worthy, they can become gods and goddesses on their own worlds. This belief views God as a union of male and female parts, a union that was dissolved when Adam and Eve left the Garden of Eden. They see polygyny as a way of restoring the fullness of the gospel and regal status of the garden. For the Allredites, Abraham and Sarah were two people who restored the state of our primal parents while on earth and serve as excellent examples for married couples beginning their "young" kingdoms.[6]

A unique aspect of this male-female union is the enveloping of plural wives into the Eve model. Allredites believe that Adam came to earth as an exalted being, having already experienced a previous earthlife when he was tested, as is every human. After that life, he returned to his father, Elohim, obtained his salvation, and became a god himself. He then went to the present earth, where he eventually married several wives, including

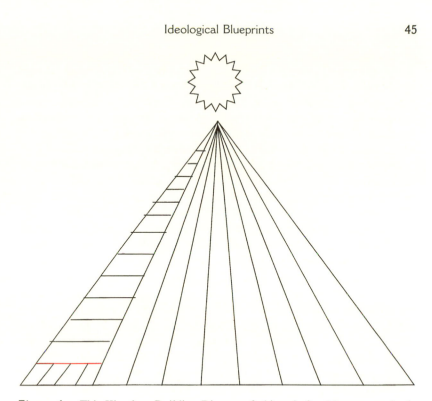

Figure 6. This Kingdom Building Diagram, fashioned after Mormon patriarch Orson Hyde's 1847 drawing, shows the order and unity of the kingdom of God. The eternal father sits at the pinnacle, crowned King of Kings and Lord of Lords. The other lines, flowing out from the pinnacle, represent a subking or priest unto God, bearing rule, authority, and dominion under the Father. Each vertical line has many horizontal lines that represent helpmeets, or wives. The smaller vertical lines attached to these represent children. When completed, the kingdom is structured to encompass many supporting subjects, all connected through the supreme patriarchal Father.

Eve and Mary, the mother of Jesus, each forming a partnership with him to create spirit children for other worlds, as they "have heretofore done."

The patriarchal order of Harker ideally establishes certain checks against the sin of men and women. A man receives a check on his righteousness by his wives, as illustrated in the story of Mary, in this chapter who has provided many women with shelter and doctrinal defense against their husbands' injustices. Mary, too, was often able to be influential in changing the course of her eternal destiny and promoting other women to take charge of their lives. Yet, this view is not generally taught or believed in Harker formal ideology. Rather, a man is never disciplined or accused by his wife unless she herself is a high-ranking member of an established family or her husband is "out of favor" with the council for some reason or other. A woman risks disfavor by exposing her lack of confidence in her husband, and she ultimately has no power to say no. All a woman can do is choose to bless the decision of her husband. This is the law.

I was told by members of the Salt Lake branch that a woman who finds her husband is unrighteous should be able to make charges of his disobedience to the council, with the idea that a correction will be made. More often than not, however, women do not complain formally; they just ask for a quick, 6-month release from the marriage. In many cases, if the conflict between spouses escalates, the family is taken over by the council. Men are rarely given opportunities to answer for their sins or the charges against them.

Women do have some recourse to control over their husbands by "blackballing" them to the council.[7] It is generally known that a woman can destroy her marriage by bad-mouthing her husband. If she is in favor with the council, she can bring almost any charge against her husband and be believed. But the opposite is true as well. A husband can condemn a wife for her injustices to him if he takes his problems to the council and they believe him. The pattern of resolutions to disputes among couples is overwhelmingly political. It all depends, one woman told me, on whom you are related to and who is most credible. For example, a Harker couple had conceived out of wedlock. A year later, after the birth of their baby, they were sealed. After a few years, the young man wanted to take a plural wife, and the wife did not trust him to conduct the courtship properly. She wanted to leave him but was counseled by her priesthood leader (a higher-ranking councilman) that she must accept the new wife without complaint. She could not accept her and wanted a release from her husband. Because they wanted an "objective view," they sought the counsel of a Salt Lake council member. He talked them into staying together, and they have remained happily married, it is said, to this day.

The difference, I was told, was that in Harker, the young wife was being "strong-armed"; no matter what she was doing, she was threatened with damnation. In the other branch, someone listened to her complaints.

Again, in general, when Harker women approach the council about the "unrighteous dominion" of their husband—that is, his abuse or neglect of them—they are often told to obey their husband's rule whether he is "in order" or not and that God would see that he "got back in order."

One woman told me that her husband was not sending any money to her to provide for new school clothes for her six children. When approached by a male leader about the shabbiness of her children's clothes, she told him that her husband had abandoned her. ''Don't speak bad of him; he is a good and righteous man'' was the leader's reply. Thus, one part of the doctrine suggests that women should be checks on their husband's righteousness, but in reality, at least in some cases, they are told to give absolute obedience and respect to him. Their only recourse is to God himself or in some cases to outside sources, an action that presents another set of problems and is considered borderline apostasy.

Harker men and women's perceptions are that they should have perfect order in their families to develop the celestial social order required in heaven. This order was explained to me in the form of a metaphor. Each family structure is like a wheel, where the hub is the priesthood head, or the husband, who is the agent of God. The spokes of the wheel are the wives, each intrinsically connected to the hub yet also connected to each other. The wheel functions properly when all spokes are straight and strong, tightly sealed to the hub. If, for any reason, the spokes or the hub detaches, the rim, which represents the family unit, will fall off, and the wheel will collapse. On a larger scale, this metaphor of order illustrates the Harker community, where the hub is the ''fullness of the gospel''— that is, the principles of righteousness, plural marriage, the United Order, and so on—and the spokes are the individual members' contributions and commitments through their stewardships or callings. The rim is the net result: the social, economic, political, and religious structure. If, for some reason, the hub is weak, the rim will deteriorate; society will collapse.

The order of heaven, as a blueprint of social structure, correlates four different gospel-oriented principles into a workable system. It is made up of the following divisions: social, political, spiritual, and economic. The social element to the heavenly order is polygyny, the political element is the kingdom of God or government of God, the spiritual element is the priesthood, and the economic element is the United Order. This order is how heaven is arranged and how Harker men and women should live today.

The doctrine further suggests that Harker men who attend church and speak in favor of polygyny are men who are willing to live its laws— laws that give men authority over their families and over ''lesser men,'' such as blacks, who are unable to live the full laws.[8] Thus, because all are to respect male authority, belief and support of the system is reciprocal and a good investment on the part of men. It promotes more power in their own priesthood and respect by women and children of that power.

Certain guidelines for men and women are quoted from the early Mormon apostle, Orson Pratt. These codes of behavior suggest that men should be good leaders, fathers, and disciplinarians. A woman should

> never seek to prejudice the mind of her husband against any of his other wives, for the purpose of exalting herself in his estimation. . . . She should try to be the peacemaker in her family and speak no evil of her husband to any of the rest of the family. She should be willing to aid the other wives in times of trouble and illness and each mother should correct her own children, and see that they do not dispute and quarrel with each other, nor with any others; let her not correct the children of the others without liberty to do so, lest they give offense. (Pratt 1874)

One of the most important examples of religious codes comes from the vision of Moroni Hancock, which relates to the correct and proper sex ratio of men and women in the kingdom of God, as attained through polygyny. This vision is part of an oral tradition that stems from the journals of early Mormon pioneers. There are virtually hundreds of stories of this type in Mormon tradition, but I have chosen the Hancock vision here to illustrate the specific differences in male and female prerogatives and progress in kingdom building. It was given to me during the first few weeks of my entrance into the group, which signifies its importance in setting up a proper understanding of the role of plural marriage in the system.

Hancock, a close friend of the Prophet Joseph Smith, was a nineteenth-century Mormon leader who was troubled by the concept of polygyny. He prayed for an answer to his question, "Why should I take another wife?" His answer was given in the form of a dream or "vision" of the heavens as they were before earthlife. He wrote that there were two lines of people forming an arc around an amphitheater in the heavens, where Jesus was giving a sermon. The male line formed the first line in the arc, facing Christ; the female line formed an arc directly in back of the male line. Thus, each female stood behind one male.

Satan appeared in the dream and began to speak. He said that he would save all those present if they would just follow him. After his speech, one-third of all present followed him to do his bidding. This one-third were all men, which left a huge surplus of women behind. Jesus commanded that each righteous man take several of the extra women and covenant to be their priesthood leader and king. The women were to align themselves to a single man, as the man's queens. The ratio of women to men in the dream correlated with the scripture found in Isaiah (4:1) so often quoted by the fundamentalists: seven to one.

In Moroni Hancock's dream, there are several key directives to converts

in their pursuit of the kingdom: Men and women have different chances
at succeeding in kingdom building; only the very few righteous men will
reap the rewards, yet an abundance of women will do so; all women sided
with the Father and the Son, whereas many men sided with the devil; and
the very elite "appointed" men will have many wives attached to them,
the unappointed righteous men will have two wives, and the unrighteous
men will have none.

Women's Place in the Order

Harker women often speak of their belief system, which often implicitly
contradicts the traditional male ideology, by emphasizing the metaphors
and rationales for the female role. The metaphor of kingdom so often used
by men, for example, is also used by a woman to enhance *her* potential
as a queen, sitting on a high and lofty throne. Part of this metaphor is the
compelling role for women to raise a large, righteous family—a family
over which *they* will rule, while their husbands are "out of the way . . .
off busy doing Priesthood business just like on earth." This personal interpretation is based on a few women's view of heaven and their rewards,
but it is nonetheless suggestive.

Women are thus promised that if they endure to the end they will be
rewarded with thrones, kingdoms, principalities, powers, dominions, glory,
immortality, and eternal lives (*Doctrine & Covenants* 75:5; 128:12, 13;
132:19, 24; Moses 1:39). These kingdoms were described to me as beautiful havens of glory where women sit on thrones alongside their husband
and share the reign of power over their children and others in their respective kingdoms, as illustrated in Mary's story. Yet women, I was told,
will not be forced to remain with an abusive or unrighteous man. If they
endure him on earth, they will be rewarded in heaven with the most honorable, choicest males.

Women also emphasize that part of Mormon doctrine which encourages
a woman to develop her talents and skills in any area of expertise. They
often quote Brigham Young's admonition to the women of his day in their
Relief Society, Young Women's classes, and informal visiting meetings.

> Women are useful not only to sweep houses, wash dishes, make beds, and
> raise babies, but that they should stand behind the counter, study law or
> physics, or become good bookkeepers and be able to do the business in any
> counting house, and all this to enlarge their sphere of usefulness for the
> benefit of society at large. In following these things they but answer the
> design of their creation. (Widstoe 1939:335)

Harker women, while cognizant of and adhering to the predominantly male ideology, have created for themselves their own versions of this ideology and structure, which are uniquely meaningful to them. They create composite profiles about the glorified status of women in various forums: Relief Society, their homes, their workplaces, and the school. For example, an extremely powerful woman, Edna, the third wife of a councilman, is allowed to attend private council meetings from time to time and is the personal secretary and confidante of the prophet. Some call her the "Eliza R. Snow of our day," and others say she is the one who actually runs the group, politically. (Eliza R. Snow was the famous second wife of Joseph Smith, who led pioneer women in their pursuit of the Kingdom of Heaven.) This woman often intervenes for councilmen in the affairs of certain families and the community as a whole and preaches the doctrine of female participation in the priesthood, which "ruffles the feathers" of many ruling elite men. She even has a bumper sticker on her car that says EVE, implying her potential for goddesshood and regality. Other role models for women are those who gain entrance into traditional male callings, such as Norma the Boy Scout leader, Jill the firehouse chief, and Liz, who was given the charge of instructing the branch on military preparedness (Liz is a former U.S. Marine). Another still is Shawna, who has been a member of the Harker City Council for several years. She has lived at the ranch for 21 years, has 13 children, and has been instrumental in many of the changes made in the school, the roads, and the water project. Rarely do these stories emerge in the company of male residents of Harker, and they are not talked about generally in religious meetings. Yet, they are a dominant feature of conversation in the informal realm of domestic activities. And finally, there is one woman chosen among them who will bless and anoint new mothers after they have conceived. This sacred ceremony is particular to women, who call upon priesthood powers to administer to other women. Women who have their second anointing can give special blessings to their own family. Some who have these special appointments go beyond the family to administer these blessings. There might be several who are qualified, for example, but only one appointed to this task.[9]

Another strengthening force in the female ideology is the recognition that polygyny provides them with respite from their husbands and male hierarchical control. The formal ideology defines plural marriage as the holy ordinance that is used to propagate the righteous seed of a righteous man, a vehicle for transporting several righteous women to heaven and building family kingdoms. The reality is that it is a practical device for enabling some women to pursue other interests and talents.[10] It also supports their independence, given this popular scripture: "In that day seven women shall take hold of one man, saying, We will eat our own bread, and wear our own apparel: only let us be called by thy name, to take away our reproach" (Isaiah 4:1).

Myth: Servant and Goddess

Harker women also share myths, very much like the biblical stories they learned as children, of how God saved them from danger, gave them the child they always dreamed of having, or caused a loved one to become well.[11] They claim that women have unique revelations not given to men. These revelations come in the form of visions of children who appear to them before their conception, requesting entrance into this world. One woman said that her daughter appeared to her as a full-grown woman with silken hair and blue eyes; she pleaded with her mother to give her a chance for earthlife. Women often share stories about the exalted, spiritual nature of their sisterhood, where all the mysteries of God will be unfolded if the sisterhood is strong enough.[12] Some women said that, if they endured the miseries and hardships of this life, they would be blessed beyond measure in the hereafter. Others go even further, saying that they could choose for themselves the man with whom they would spend an eternity, not necessarily their earthly husband. In fact, one woman is certain that she will be given Joseph Smith himself as a husband. Often these metaphors and myths are in the form of daydreams to make life seem better than it is. Another woman said that learning to share becomes a heavenly art, an art perfected by women. Men have such a difficult time sharing and doing charity work that they will be minimally provided for in the hereafter, as punishment.

These stories are accompanied by tearful testimonials of the "truthfulness of the gospel" and God's mercy. They are binding tools to unite opposing personality types, age barriers, or jealousies among sisterwives. If any woman does not easily join these spiritual sessions (Relief Society meeting or Joseph Smith Pageant) with the accompanying tears and expressions of joy, she is thought by some to be a nonbeliever and is not often extended the same friendship and help in the networking system.

In these sharing sessions, which can take place during Relief Society meetings, Sunday meetings, and informal visiting sessions, women repeat the story of Mary and Martha, the two dearest friends of Jesus (Luke 10: 38–39). In fundamentalist belief, Jesus married both Mary and Martha, because he loved them both (John 11:5). And because the two sisters loved each other dearly, they, with their husband, became a loving eternal round.

The character of Martha, a woman who was devoted to her home and family duties, is a canon for household magnificence for Harker women. Mary, too, was given gifts—gifts of a different sort, which gave her the ability to conduct affairs outside the home. She is the model for women who work in the marketplace. These two sisters, devoted as they were to their talents and to their families, were the perfect combination.

Mother Eve represents another myth that women apply to themselves. Eve is the supreme example of righteousness. Adam held the priesthood, Eve was the mother of all living, and they were a team. Because of this perfect model, each wife may join with her husband as a partner unified in purpose (1 Corinthians 11:11). Like Eve, each woman must welcome children into her life and nurture them. She must be obedient to the commandment to multiply and replenish the earth, which is her glory and her reward.

The mere existence of a goddess in a Harker pantheon does not necessarily suggest an exalted position for women. On the contrary, the status of goddess is still beneath the status of male "god." What is important about the myth of goddesshood, however, is how this myth affects the way women feel about themselves and the unity it brings to their relations with each other. One woman suggested that, as on earth, heaven will be set up with busy husbands (gods) attempting to rule several kingdoms, spreading their thin authority over a large sovereignty. On earth, women will be in charge of their own respective family kingdoms, as sovereigns over their own children. There is an apparent paradox in Harker between the symbolic ascendancy of women and their social denigration or inferiority. Yet, for women who believe in their potential as sovereigns of kingdoms, this paradox seems to go unnoticed and is unimportant. Women will suffer for a good cause, and the cause of attaining goddesshood, with all their children lifted up to heaven with them, is the greatest cause of all. It is often said that women, who for so long were denied their right to the powers they deserved as "half of the whole," have stifled their participation in the priesthood. Those who recognize their true calling and divine right to priesthood blessings exercise these rights in quiet.

The "pain and suffering" motif, which Max Weber (1930) said was the motivation for religious belief, is used continually in Harker female ideology. For example, women often tell stories of their pioneer past, when their own mothers, grandmothers, and great-grandmothers were humbled in raising their children under adverse conditions. In these stories, such as the one about Widow X who saved her ox by anointing him with sacred oil, women are a powerful force in the settlement of the West. They are seen to be righteous stewards of their families in all their "Spartan strength of character," as obedient "servants" to their husbands and children. The more vivid the details of hardship, sacrifice, and surrender, the better—to emphasize the strengths and rewards of the female "saints," in contrast to perhaps the historical fact of pioneer women's actual denigration at the hands of their husbands. These pioneer stories reinforce their own suffering and enlist a view of a heaven that is worth any price or pain.

One woman quoted to me the famous writings of James Tullidge (1877), an early Mormon historian, who compiled statements made about women of early Mormonism.

> In the past the apostleship of woman has not been fairly granted to her, even among the most civilized nations. But it shall be; and there is the hope of the world . . . if woman's spiritual nature prevail not in the church, then is the church dead. If her faith expires, then is there left but a wretched form of godliness . . . woman must regenerate the race by endowing it with more of her own nature. She must bring forth a better type of man, to work out with her a better civilization . . . she shall leaven the earth with her own nature . . . in her great office of maternity, and in her apostolic mission. (541–544)

What this quotation means to many in the Allred group is that they shall triumph over the evil in the world through their unique powers as *females*, not necessarily in their capacity as wives and mothers.

Women's Voices in Ideology

The following narratives are based on interviews of 12 different women compiled into three "voices" that are prototypical of Harker women's experiences. The first voice, Jan's, is most commonly found among women who are high-ranking first and second wives of established family men or are highly trained to perform a service that is valued in the society, such as midwifery, Relief Society presidency, female spokesperson for the group or branch, and organizer of firesides (a special evening meeting) and educational programs. It is difficult to tell how common the second narrative voice is. It is a combination of three women who have experienced feelings of alienation from their husbands and other male priesthood holders and have, through desperation and frustration, found their own sense of priesthood power. My observation is that this narrative (Liz's voice) represents very few women in Harker but is vital in understanding some of the coping strategies of women who are isolated from priesthood help. The third narrative, Mary's story, represents a growing number of women who have "altered" the traditional fundamentalist doctrine to meet their sociological and psychological needs. This type of woman is often used to being in charge of programs and projects and predominantly comes from the mainstream Mormon church.

These narratives alone do not represent the women of Harker as a whole, on the contrary, some women disagree with Mary's version of kingdom building or have never experienced Liz's sense of power. Yet, I suggest that composite profiles like these are circulated around the community and create metaphoric innovations and new constructs of belief that convey a sense of influence and self-worth. These personalized versions of Harker theology are not necessarily the formal doctrines of the Allred group, but, rather, individuals' attempts to mesh their experiences and hopes with their beliefs.

Jan

Jan is 65 years old. She is 5 foot, 10 inches tall and has blond hair and bright blue eyes. She is one of the most powerful, influential women in the Allred group, although not always outspoken in the presence of men, especially her husband, Bob, who is the second most powerful man in Harker. Her name is often associated with the "divine character of goddesshood" and "the role model for women of the sect."

Jan and has given birth to 17 children, 15 of whom are living. This quantity gives her a great deal of prestige because women who bring more spirits down from heaven are saving souls and guaranteeing their place in the next life as queens and sovereigns. Jan is the first wife of a prominent council member and has four "sisterwives," all of whom defer to her decision-making control. She is the community's midwife, ob-gyn, nursemaid, doctor, herbalist, and childcare specialist. Her home was built with a large master bedroom suite, which is her naturopathic office during the day and her sleeping area at night. She designed her home and gave the plans to her husband to build it. It is an extremely well-built, comfortable home. She provides an extensive prenatal and postnatal program for community women, which includes several checkups and herbal treatments. Jan delivers 95% of the community's babies, by last count nearly a thousand Allred group children.

She began her midwife training as an apprentice to the former prophet, Rulon Allred, also a naturopath. As young as age 14, she watched him deliver babies under the most challenging of circumstances, with healing hands and the power of the priesthood as his primary tools. She said she uses these same techniques in her own practice. In fact, she was the first woman I ever knew who actually called on priesthood powers to bless someone by "the laying on of hands and anointing with oil." She was appointed to this high calling by the former prophet, Rulon.[13]

Jan usually charges each of her patients for some of the costs of her services, totaling no more than $75, and personally absorbs any additional costs. Jan herself receives no income for this service and is on call 24 hours a day for visits, checkups, nutritional analyses, and deliveries. During the actual delivery, ideally, the patient's sister or co-wife will attend her. A priesthood bearer, usually the husband, will also be present. It is not uncommon for 6 to 8 individuals to witness the birth of a child, which is one of the most celebrated events in the community. Jan said that childbirth was often an effective bonding experience among women. Pregnancy, childbirth, nursing, and childcare are experiences that *all* have and thus the "safest" areas in which to find commonalities. Quite often, a woman's co-wife is the only one available to help her during her recovery from childbirth by taking care of her children and making sure that she has enough wood cut for a warm fire and enough food for her needs.

As part of the prenatal regimen, Jan requires mothers to take vitamins and do exercises throughout their pregnancy and to drink a quart of raspberry and/or comfrey tea every day to prevent hemorrhaging and aid in the delivery. She also has the mothers eat alfalfa for vitamin D during pregnancy. For toxemia, she uses snake grass, corn silk, or parsley. If she has "a bleeder on her hands," she gives them bioflavinoids—the white part of grapefruit, orange, or lemon.

The birthing procedure varies from woman to woman but is usually conducted in a woman's own bedroom. When the contractions are approximately 5 minutes apart, a woman calls the midwife and lies down on her bed to await her arrival. When Jan arrives, she calls on God's help to bring about a safe delivery and begins making the woman more comfortable with massage and perhaps something warm to drink. Sometimes in the process of difficult labor, Jan manually reaches in and stimulates the cervix, or turns the baby, if tipped. She said that this technique is unheard of in hospital obstetrics, but it works wonderfully for her, and she never performs C-sections.[14] If a woman is hemorrhaging, Jan bestows a healing prayer on the woman and asks for the priesthood to administer to her.[15] She then has the mother drink blue cohosh, *Caulophyllum thalictroides,* which helps clot the blood and also helps the placenta pass more quickly through the canal. Chinese herbs are also used in hemorrhaging. She manually massages the uterus after the birth to stop the bleeding. She also binds the mother after birth with a towel or other wrap around the uterus. She folds the towel in front so it will weigh down the uterus. She learned this practice from Rulon Allred and swears by it, but she says that no other midwife uses this practice.

Jan actively participates in sacred priesthood rituals. In fact, she simultaneously draws from two vital sources of priesthood power—the Melchizedek priesthood that she shares with her husband and the creative processes of birth, which she shares with God. Jan is symbolic of how women's powers are demonstrated in the patriarchal system.[16] She is a woman who essentially performs the task or miracle herself, often without the help of men. But in order to draw on the Spirit and the powers of heaven, she must be connected to a true priesthood conduit—her husband. As his eternal mate, he provides her with the Melchizedek priesthood, and she provides him with access to the celestial kingdom. No man can enter the highest glory unless he is sealed to a righteous woman.

Jan has many sources of power in Harker. She is the first wife of one of the most powerful men in the entire group. She is a trained naturopath and midwife, and thus the center of all medical knowledge of the branch. Plus, she has her "second anointings," which make her, literally, a queen of a legitimate earthly kingdom. Whether her husband lives or dies at this point, she will retain her symbolic and material powers in the branch. "God speaks through her to us," as one woman said. In short, Jan is a prototype of the perfect Harker woman—a role model for all other women to follow.

Liz

Liz is 55 years old, has long brown hair usually tucked in a bun, and is 5 foot, 7 inches tall. Although she was an active and powerful member of the Allred group for more than 25 years, she is no longer a member. Years ago, when she lived in Harker with her husband and six children, she found it very difficult to cope with illnesses and the scarcity of resources during the absence of her husband, who often worked in construction in another state. She is her husband's second wife and has an especially good relationship with the elderly first wife.

She remembers a very difficult time, several years back, when her feverish child needed a priesthood blessing. The 8-year-old boy could hardly breathe and could not keep down any food. His temperature soared above 103; she knew he was dying. The boy had whooping cough, a disease that was especially bad in the Bitterroot area that year. With five other children to care for and her husband not available, she asked one of the councilmen to give her son a special blessing to live and rid his body of all toxins, the normal procedure for women in need. The councilman in charge did not come, though she waited and waited. Nor did he send another man to help. The council leadership had been busy with calls to bless many other children, as the epidemic had spread throughout the community. Her own husband was in Oregon on business, as usual. Rather than draw on the priesthood powers that she shared through her husband, she said she went to the Lord *directly*. She had seen other women do this, over the years, and was confident that she would be able to work with the Lord in healing her boy.

> I gathered my five children together around the bed of my boy and said, "It's time for us to pray," and I laid my hands on his head and gave him a mother's blessing. I just pled to God to let him live. I then anointed his head with holy oil.[17] And asked God to make him healthy. Within 15 minutes, he was sitting up and asking for food.

Liz said she was sure of her own power as a conduit for the priesthood powers. She felt the power of God surge through her body and enter the body of her son. The room was alight, and there was a strange warmth to it. She felt so strange, and yet the experience was so familiar. The idea that she could actually heal her son! It was a miracle! This experience and many others like it caused Liz to pause and think, "What is so special about *male* priesthood?" She began to speak to other women of her experience, and together they formed an informal group of sisters who believed in the rightful powers of female priesthoods. These women emphasized the Gnostic and Hebrew versions of the Adam-Eve story, which presented the scenario of male-female unity. Long ago, as the scenario goes, Adam and Eve were connected both spiritually and physically. Their voices were one voice; their minds one mind. After the sin of the forbidden fruit, patriarchies and matriarchies began to develop throughout the world, separating the two souls. Females have just as much right to the gifts of priesthood that God has given them because he gave it to them when they were "one" with Adam. Even though they are not formally in charge of priesthood rites and powers, in that they are separated from Adam, they are still powerfully connected to their gifts and have the right to perform many ceremonies and healings.

For 10 more years, Liz stayed in the group and continued to heal her children and others' children with her priesthood powers. Since Liz left the group because she had a falling out with the leaders of the group she has had a different perspective of women's role in the Allred group. She suggests that most women are slaves to the male system and do not realize their own powers. Her relationship with her husband had been shaky since

the very beginning, which may have contributed to her decision to "apostate." Yet, in spite of this sentiment, she talks fondly of the times when
she discovered, through the absence of her husband, her own powers to
bless and heal her children. "I just feel bad I never told enough women
about it," she said. "I was afraid that the council would find out."

Liz feels that though there are many women who believe as she does,
they will not be able to practice openly many of the priesthood rites that
are performed formally by men. It would disrupt the control the men have
over the women, she said. Nonetheless, she attests to the value of the
underground belief system as a way for women to gain autonomy and
control over their lives.

"I would never have recognized my own power, had I been in a monogamous relationship in the mainstream chruch," she recalls. "I had to
be in a position where I was frightened, alone, and desperate. That can
only happen in polygamy where the husband is always out of town . . . he
was never there for me . . . never around when I truly needed him. I was
forced to discover the power within me . . . out of necessity I found my
true self."

Mary

Mary is the 68-year-old third wife of a plumber who is from an established
group family and has three other wives. He lives in another state. Mary
is 5 foot, 1 inch tall and has gray hair and brown eyes. In spite of her
slight height, she is a powerful speaker and has a strong personality that
says, "Do not mess with me. You'll regret it!" She has a natural cynicism
toward newcomers but is attracted to new ideas and loves discussing intellectual issues about Mormonism. She is a member of the Harker town
council, teaches the adult Sunday school class, and instructs eight junior
high and high school students in computer science, mathematics, religious
philosophy, history, and English literature from her home. Her current
pride and joy is the new addition to her barnlike house, which provides
her with one extra bedroom and bath and houses a small computer class-
room for her students. Her ability to research any topic at short notice is
well known, and many Harker residents consider her to be something of
a "women's libber." She is knowledgeable on almost any bit of gossip
in the Allred group, and has formed an informal group of disgruntled
women who, she says, "have no one else to talk to about their problems."

One woman described Mary as the watchdog for the injustices pefor-
med by men on woman in the group. Another resident told me that she
is a catalyst for breaking up families in order to be popular among women.

Others told me that she provided them with a voice when they felt stifled and alone. One council member implied that she was a threat to the strength of the celestial order. Her mobilization of women encourages many wives to "take matters into their own hands."

Mary's most unusual facet, however, is her interpretation of the gospel of Jesus Christ. It motivates her to help other women in trouble, teach children to love and not fear the Principle, and keep a constant check on the community. She can often be heard discussing with men and some women deep and difficult nuances about the doctrine such as blood atonement, goddesshood, divine descent, and "saviors on Mt. Zion," always emphasizing women's role in the divine plan. She has no doubt that women are destined for greatness and believes that an eternal throne is awaiting her at the end of this life.

Mary believes that *women*, not men, have the final decision in the composition of a family kingdom because not only do they bear and raise the subjects of this kingdom but also they have the power to remove them from a kingdom; that is, women can train their children toward the dark side if they so choose. Women are the ones who ultimately have the right to deny any unrighteous man the control over themselves and their children. Her judgments of men are that they, for the most part, are "seekers of gold and flesh; incapable of their holy task." She said it is well known that it is much harder for men to live the principle than it is for women.

When she was 23, Mary had a vision of marrying a prominent council member, saying that she knew he was the one. The man had a few differences of opinion with Mary, but he had to consider her proposal. During this time, she asked another council member, saying that she had a vision of him, too, and eventually she married the second council member.

Many years ago, when this council member died, she decided who she would remarry and told the matchmaker that she wanted the plumber. She said she used a number of economic and ideological criteria in making this decision. Because she had six young children already, she sought someone who was established in the community, had a good business, had experience with plural living (he already had two wives), understood what it took to be a good father, and honored his priesthoods. In Harker, when a woman chooses a man, the council supports her decision and sanctions the plural marriage. So, Mary chose her man, and now she gets to choose her eternal line of descent for herself and her children.

As the former wife of a deceased councilman (the son of the former prophet, Rulon), she has a unique position in the eternal line of descent, although there is some concern over this councilman's eternal ranking (he committed suicide). As third wife to the mayor, her second husband, her celestial position is also enhanced, as he is a "good and righteous man" who obeys the Lord and is "strong in his priesthoods." He is, however, a convert, who is not directly descended of polygynist stock, which poses a problem in her celestial schema.

Because Mary is closely related to the current prophet through her mother's father's line, she has decided that she will be connected to neither of her husbands' lines and instead graft onto her matrilineal connections to exaltation. She explained to me that I must decide which line to graft onto because my husband was not in the Principle (neither was I, for that matter). After examining my genealogy, she suggested that I graft onto my great-grandfather Israel Bennion, or my great-grandfather George M. Cannon, as they were the last polygynists of the family. I left that interview with the distinct flavor of being in charge of my eternal life! I can imagine just how powerfully Mary's liberal interpretation of the divine female role affects other women in the community.

She told me that women should be practicing on earth for being royal sovereigns of their dynasties in heaven and that she fully expects to be rewarded with "crowns, thrones, and principalities" (*Doctrine & Covenants* 75:5), as nothing prohibits a woman from obtaining these things.

THESE COMPOSITE PROFILES about the lives of Jan, Liz, and Mary tell us a great deal about the ways women tap into patriarchal Mormon ideology. Women are actually shaping and directing their belief system. Their interpretations of the doctrine and their contributions to society through ritual significantly enhance their progression in kingdom building. In fact, upon analyzing the involvement of men and women in religiopolitical rituals and callings, I found a striking difference. Table 1 illustrates the religiopolitical status of converts in a sample of 110 individuals (75 fe-

Table 1.   Religio-political Status among Male and Female Converts

Position/Status	Males	Females
Administrative calling*	4 (11.4%)	10 (13.3%)
Councilman's wife or male-female appointee	5 (14.3%)	20 (26.7%)
Endowments	12 (34.3%)	40 (53.3%)
Informal spiritual calling	14 (40.0%)	5 (6.7%)
Total	35	75

*Although many of these statuses are not mutually exclusive—that is, one can hold an administrative position and have endowments, too—I have categorized individuals based on their *dominant* calling or status, which is the one that they are known by most people to hold.

males, 35 males) from 1989 to 1993. It shows a slightly higher percentage of converts (13.3% or 10 of 75) within the domain of "administrative calling," which includes such positions as supervisors, teachers, leaders, and other female appointee placements, than male converts in this same domain. These are the callings that Jan and Mary hold in the community.

The most significant area of spiritual resource disparity, however, was in the close contact with elite leaders and the participation in endowments. A higher percentage of women (26.7% or 20 of 75) than were men (14.3% or 5 of 35) were either married to councilmen or assigned to be their adoptees, which gave them a significant headstart in their progress. And 54% of the female converts (40 out of 75) have access to sacred ordinances and rites associated with the endowment house, which only 34.3% men (12 out of 35) have. Women do not have to be spiritual giants or be outspoken in the gospel to attend the endowment house. They need only be married, and that requirement enables all women in Harker to attend. Finally, note that almost all women (93.3%) advanced above the level of "informal spiritual calling," while a substantial percentage of male converts (40%) had *not* advanced above this basic status level.

Another measure of religiopolitical status besides endowment participation is achievement of the "second anointing." These ordinances are sacred and were kept formally secret, but when I asked who had these high-ranking priesthood blessings, my informants seemed to be aware of exactly who had received them. Jan was among the few women who admitted to have held this position. I was told that more women than men have their second anointings because their husbands, whether dead or alive, have been blessed with this great rank, and by association they, too, gain the rank. Also, prominent men with second anointings usually have many wives, increasing the overall number of females with this rank.

Furthermore, women have an informal set of rites associated with bearing and rearing children that is not accessible to men. When a woman knows she is to have a child, she goes to the midwife and finds out whether she is healthy and how far along the pregnancy is. She then gains a special "mother's blessing" from a high-ranking woman who has received her second anointing. This prominent woman blesses and anoints the woman in a special ceremony that is attended by only women. She blesses the mother with good general health, with emphasis on a safe delivery of the child. She blesses her with courage and strength and the Spirit of Christ to attend her.

In sum, the distribution of spiritual resources among men and women suggests the following patterns.

1. Approximately 70% of those able to access the endowment house were female; this same percentage includes those who are blessed by the Holy Spirit of Promise during celestial marriage.
2. Women have informal or vicarious access to symbolic rituals through marital relationships with established elites.
3. Nonelite men have limited formal access to symbolic prestations, such as rituals, positions, and ceremonies.

Summary

Harker ideology, whether interpreted by men or women, is a force in society that separates male and female roles and spheres of influence. Men control the formal ideological and political aspects of community living, but women manage and influence the more basic aspects of day-to-day survival. The Harker worldview is comprised of a complementary and contradictory relationship between male ideology and female reality: priesthood and motherhood, the head and the body, the sovereign and the servant, the power and the support system for that power.

The ideological effect on female advantage is so great that it needs to be seen as a phase in the progression model. While phase one showed the male-female difference in motivations to join the group and the tensions accompanying conversion, phase two (figure 7) deals with the issues that individuals face once baptized and officially committed to the group. This second step in the kingdom-building process is the stage of indoctrination, which is the thorough instruction given to converts throughout the first months (and often years) of their entrance into the group. This instruction initially stresses an explicit understanding of the important rules that converts must follow in their journey to exaltation. It then concentrates on indoctrination of several key ideological tenets that are represented in prominant myths and symbols, the most important of which is the concept of the covenant. Finally, it emphasizes the learning and adoption of key role models that provide additional guides in kingdom building. Together, these rules, myths, symbols, and role models comprise the ideal codes that are vital in playing the kingdom-building game. The male and female converts who are able to answer "yes" to obeying rules and adapting scripts, are able to move onto the next level, of filling roles. I should note that some converts know more about ideological tenets than others do and begin to use their knowledge as early as investigation to the group. Others take years to absorb all the subtleties of the ideology.

In sum, rules, scripts, and roles provide more ironies and missteps for male converts than it does for female converts. Inequalities and competi-

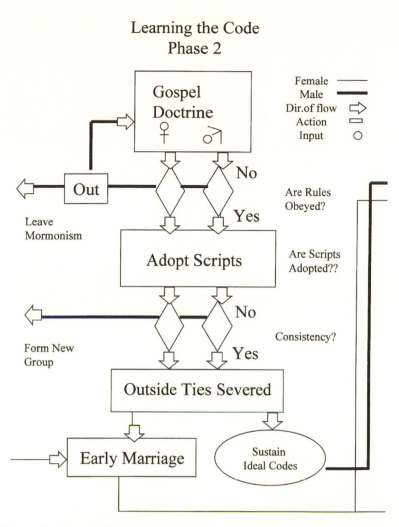

Learning the Code
Phase 2

Gospel Doctrine ♀ ♂

Female ————
Male ▬▬▬
Dir.of flow ⇨
Action ▭
Input ○

Out

Leave Mormonism

No

Are Rules Obeyed?

Yes

Adopt Scripts

Are Scripts Adopted??

No

Form New Group

Consistency?

Yes

Outside Ties Severed

Early Marriage

Sustain Ideal Codes

Figure 7. Phase 2 shows how male and female converts become indoctrinated, requiring them to pass through additional tests, such as obeying council and community rules, adopting appropriate roles or "scripts," and then fulfilling these roles adequately. Here, too, the females are more likely than males to pass these tests and move on to the next phase of instruction.

tion mostly affect men in kingdom building; rewards are more consistent for women. The diagram of male-female progress in kingdom building (figure 7) shows how women often sidestep the formal observance of rules and roles by marrying directly into a high-ranking family or by bringing in children from a previous marriage. At the point of conversion, women are entering the group for vastly different reasons, centered in the reality of their socioeconomic needs. They readily adopt the formal rules and roles that are ascribed to them, while informally developing a hidden ideology that strengthens their belief in female divinity and progress. In short, high-status women have more power than low-status men. Women's agency is clear here; they can act on their own ideology for advantage, as the cases clearly show.

four

＊

Economic Challenges and Creative Financing

How Judith Got By on $76 a Month

Women provide food and shelter for themselves and their families through creative financing, outside employment, and female communalism. Female converts tend to do better than male converts in accessing communal resources and providing for their families through informal channels. This chapter provides a brief socioeconomic background of converts and examines the nature of male-female earning power and relative access to valued resources. It concludes by describing how some women are able to provide for themselves in the face of incredible odds.

Socioeconomic Background of Converts

In analyzing the characteristics of converts' histories, I found that of the 1,024 converts who initially joined the group, only 69% (706) had graduated from high school. Of that number, 12% (143) had earned a college degree, and 23% (236) had attended college. Overall, blue-collar labor was the most common profession (35% or 358 individuals), with a smaller percentage in the occupations of manufacturer (12% or 82 individuals), teacher (21% or 215 individuals), administrator (6% or 61 individuals), and salesperson (26% or 266 individuals).

Conversion to the Allred group for women was followed by striking upward social and economic mobility. Several women earned their bachelor's degrees in education and nursing at local colleges and institutes upon joining the group. More important, *all* women in the sample who wished to marry did so, in most cases to highly prestigious established

65

Table 2.   Employment Advancement before and after Joining the Group

	Before		After	
	No. of Males	No. of Females	No. of Males	No. of Females
Full-time	17 (48.6%)	10 (13.3%)	12 (34.2%)	26 (34.6%)
Part-time	12 (34.2%)	20 (26.6%)	9 (25.7%)	32 (42.6%)
Unemployed	6 (17.1%)	45 (60.0%)	14 (40.0%)	17 (22.6%)
Total	35 (100%)	75 (100%)	35 (100%)	75 (100%)

leaders. The greatest social mobility has occurred among single, educated women in their 30s, who join the group and marry members of the high council or their appointees. Table 2 shows the discrepancy between 35 men and 75 women in terms of employment and educational advancement. This sample of 110 individuals is not randomly drawn but, rather, is a selection of men and women from the Harker and Zion orders who expressed a wide range of characteristics, containing a representative number of converts and established male and female individuals who were in all types of economic and social categories. Furthermore, this sample contains individuals with whom I lived and worked on a daily, personal basis, and I can therefore attest to the accuracy of my information. The table shows that women who were usually unemployed prior to entering the group (60% unemployment) were somehow able to secure at least part-time work after joining the order (22.6% unemployment). Men, however, found that after quitting or losing their previous jobs to be polygynists, they could not find work as members of the group (40% unemployment). This difference may be due to the common practice of women's use of their maiden names after marriage to cloak their involvement, whereas males are usually labeled polygynists to employers very quickly in all branches of the group. Socioeconomic advancement is one of many factors that relate to successful integration in this study.

Conversion to fundamentalism offers a unique social, economic, and spiritual experience for most women—one that the mainstream Mormon church does not. The Allred group provides a milieu in which lower-class female recruits can ascend to a position of higher marriage (hypergamy) and can attain a higher level of economic satisfaction than do lower-class male recruits. They also tend to create and manage their own domestic areas, where they have significant influence over their children and their subsistence. Once there, however, polygynist women face serious "circumscriptive'' barriers that prohibit them from leaving the sect,[1] whereas low-ranking young men,[2] particularly those born into convert families, are encouraged to leave. It is not always out of satisfaction, then, that women remain in the group. Some remain because their options on the outside are few.

Harker operates on a *partial* communal system. Because no one in Harker pays either rent or mortgage payments (all land and homes are communally owned) and there are no medical insurance bills to pay, no central heating (all homes are heated by wood stoves) or outside water bills, the monthly expenses for one family can be quite low. Harker has the lowest tax base in the state, and there are no city taxes. The water used in each home is gathered from the natural streams and rivers of the mountains into two water boxes near the mouths of two canyons. Each extended family is charged $10 per family for water per month. At present, only one-third of the town is paying this amount; the rest are getting their water free. All of this adds up to a system that is much like the moshavim of Israel, where individual industry is combined with communally owned housing and land. In this semicommunal system, families can survive using wage labor, out-of-the house sales, construction contracts, the female network, and creative financing. A woman often must manage her own finances independent of her husband's income or even charity from the priesthood.

In such a system, women in a financial bind who are waiting for the next paycheck (or government welfare check), can get by through the help of other women who have passed their crises. In some cases, there is an element of ''tolerated theft'' involved in this sharing of goods and services. Blurton Jones (1987) invented this term to account for hunter-gatherer sharing tactics, in which an individual allows theft or does not begrudge the request of *less* valuable resources that are needed by someone else.

Jane, a Harker woman who relies heavily on the economic sharing of goods, stated that the community itself would not be sustained without sisterwife cooperation. She said that the school would not stand without this networking and that women do community projects that are just as important, though not as visible, as those of the men. They fix up the interior of new houses, repair, sew, bake, care for the sick, cook supper for a whole family for a week, can fruit and vegetables for several wives for the entire winter, and care for others' children. She personally cooperates with her sisterwife by sharing every item and household good in the house. The income provided by her sisterwife, who works as a store clerk, and her husband, who works in construction, is enough to sustain them financially. Jane's part is to care for the children and maintain the home. When her sisterwife works the night shift, the kids are under Jane's care, and when Jane teaches kindergarten at the school once in a while, her sisterwife watches Jane's kids.

Not all women, however, engage in cooperative economic networking; in fact, women often said that under normal circumstances—that is, no poverty, no sharing of husband and his possessions, and the like—there would be little contact between co-wives whatsoever. "She is the last person on this earth I would ask for help," said one woman about her co-wife, indicating that payback between co-wives is rough. There is also underlying competition and attempts to outdo the other.

Jobs

Many women must take on jobs outside the community for the family to survive. In a sample of 50 working women, I found that 21 had a full-time position such as nurse, secretary, schoolteacher, clerk, accountant, or housecleaner. Yet, among these, only 8 earned fully competitive salaries outside Harker. The others, many of them working at the school, store, or post office, were full employees of the communal system, receiving less than $40 a month. One sold Amway products from her home. The other 26 working women were engaged in part-time work in both community and marketplace jobs. Calculating the exact value of community labor to the community, and household labor to the family is difficult, as these women's jobs are not valued by the hierarchy, and the income is often given directly over to expenses. Fewer Harker women work full-time than work part-time and community-type jobs, which enables more women to share the tasks of managing their households with other community-bound women. By contrast, men are able to share their occupational tasks with other men.

Most men are skilled in construction, metalworking, and woodworking, and other blue-collar trades. These men work long hours, almost entirely outside the community, and in some cases move out of state for the winter to secure work. Male high school students are part-time members of the local work pool and may be assigned specific tasks such as cutting wood, cleaning tools, or repairing machinery. They gather at the church two Saturdays a month for communal projects, which include labor on the water boxes, new buildings and houses, and machinery. The husband's primary role is provider, yet the role is extended to the task of being the spiritual and theological receptor from God to his family through the priesthood. Along with their employment, the men must contribute free labor to community projects that require skills in building, farming, buying, selling, and record keeping. These labor projects, however, are far and few between. Most of their working hours—8 to 10 hours a day—are spent at their place of employment, away from their community, wives, and families.

Thus, Harker male and female earning power can be seen to be quite different but complementary. Not all women work, just as not all men work. Some are freeloading off the priesthood funds under the title of retired or widowed or unemployed. Some women are associated with writing and research; some men are involved in history or doctrine work. However, most women must work, in some context or another, whether at an outside, high-paying salaried job, at a community, low-paying school position, or at home, tending children and managing the household. Women are obviously not in the same class as men in terms of occupations that earn regular salaries, but because there are so many women in the community, the hours they do earn are significant in illustrating their economic interdependence and contribution to family income and community stability. On average, Harker women work 25 to 30 hours per week outside their homes in either community or marketplace work. On average, a Harker man works 40 to 55 hours per week at his job and 5 to 15 hours per week on community and church-related jobs. These figures do not succeed in tracing the exact nature of women's work at home, but they do show that women, because of their large numbers, spend more time collectively, but not individually, than men do.[3] In this context, I would call this labor ''social production'' (Sacks 1974), in which women contribute to the production of community life, the subsistence of the family, and the production of the next generation of laborers through reproduction.

The allocation of family economic resources is based on the number of children per wife per husband. Ideally, each head of family is responsible for ensuring that all of his wives are caring for and providing for their children. In reality, because of his frequent absence from home, it is up to each individual wife to manage her household and provide for her children what is not already provided them by their father. To accomplish this, she relies on whatever measures she can to get the needed items, such as shoplifting for April or welfare for Gretchen, as seen in this chapter. More often, however, she uses the winter stores supplied through her cooperative efforts with her co-wives and other women of the community, like Judith. Another common tactic is to save money by using many different natural cures before taking their children to see a physician or by using the money saved for food or clothing for other necessities. Although many wives do not want to ask for help when ill, there is usually some female member of the community who helps cut wood, provides a loaf of bread, or watches the children for a certain time.[4]

Differential access to material resources is also dependent on the distribution of lower stewardships and the sexual division of labor among the general population. All members of the community, both male and female, have economic and social stewardships. Women perform a wider range of valued tasks in the more rural settings, such as Harker, because husbands are more often absent, seeking employment in the larger communities. Women are forced into the independence that hones new skills and necessitates a wider range of chores. Harker women do not make more money than Salt Lake City women. On the contrary, urban women have a tendency to be more educated and have higher wages than rural women, but, again, the rural women have a wider range of subsistence-related skills.

To make ends meet, many polygynous women and their children must take jobs outside the community. In a sample of 75 working women (40 established, 35 convert), I found that 41.4% (10 established and 21 convert) were involved in full-time employment (table 3). These women worked in such positions as nurse, secretary, schoolteacher, clerk, accountant, and housecleaner. Of the remaining 44 women, 27 (17 established, 10 convert) worked as part-time employees both inside and outside the community in such positions as school custodian, librarian, store clerk, post office clerk, and hotel night clerk. As previously stated, one woman sold Amway products from her home. Another cleaned houses 2 days a week. Still another sold herbal products, bringing in $50 to $80 a week. Of those 17 that were formally unemployed, 13 were established women, and only four were convert. These numbers indicate that fewer established women work in the marketplace but find other ways of bringing in money through "creative" part-time labor in the community. The data also suggest that convert women are more highly trained (more years

Table 3. Employment Status of Allredite Women

Women	Employment Categories among Women				
	Mean Years of Education	Number Working Part-Time	Number Working Full-Time	Unemployed	Total
Convert	13.5	10 (28.6%)	21 (60.0%)	4 (11.4%)	35
Established	10.5	17 (42.5%)	10 (25.0%)	13 (32.5%)	40
Total		27 (36.0%)	31 (41.4%)	17 (22.6%)	75

Table 4.   Economic Status among Male and Female Converts by Type

Type of Resource	Males	Females
Property/Industry Stewardship	11 (32%)	29 (38%)
Salaried labor		
Professional	5 (15%)	13 (17%)
Unskilled	19 (53%)	33 (45%)
Total	35	75

of education) and provide more money for their families than do established women.

This review of male and female community economic activities suggests that most men worked outside the community and often out of state and that their absence from the homefront had a direct impact on female economic activities. Women are considered by the community to be forced into an interdependence with each other and are often expected to provide for the families in the absence of their husbands, especially if he has other wives outside the community. When men leave their wives for long periods, the women are more dependent on each other for economic and emotional support. This interdependence among wives is similar to the split labor found in many African polygynous cultures, such as the Zulu. Table 4 shows the relative occupational status—the type of *formal* employment that someone has, not including *informal* creative financing outside the work force—of husbands and wives in the 110-convert sample. It is merely one measure of of differential access to valued material resources among converts. In this sample of 110 individuals, there are as many or more in both the property/industrial stewardship and salaried labor categories. For example, 5 of 35 husbands are employed in a professional occupation, but 13 of 75 wives hold professional positions in the workplace, mostly in nursing.[5]

Those who do not utilize the economic network have other means of securing food and clothing for their families. In a survey of 15 families, 7 of them did not participate in the female network, and of those 7, 3 received ample funds from their husband's income, and 4 relied on government welfare. As one women put it, "Sometimes it is easier to go to welfare than ask your husband or sistewives for help—it is often the best solution."

"It is out of desperation that we cooperate," said one woman. "We all keep our ears and eyes open for bargains, and know what everyone will need and get it for them when the moment arrives." One woman said that she and her husband brought a huge trailer of rice for everyone in the community. "The hard times just brought us together," she said.

This subtle system of reciprocity and quasi-communal exchange can be best understood by statements often made by both men and women about their involvement in the United Order. (The United Order is the groups' financing structure, modeled after the original Mormon rule of consecration of goods and services.) "Women are much better sharers than men are. Men get hung up on material status and making more money. Women are just trying to survive . . . not rule the financial world," said one female informant.

In sum, Harker residents use the United Order to minimize privileged position and private gain. Ideally, the United Order will achieve this through the honest and full consecration of tithes and offerings, the complete surrender of time and energy, the communal distribution of goods and services, the storage and rotation of new and used goods; and the equal provision of surplus to the poor and needy. In reality, most men cannot feed and clothe all the children, much less their wives, especially in the impoverished Bitterroot area. They are often not around to help and, when they do contribute, it has to be divided among the different households. To deal with the unpredictability in material resources, women have to find work outside the community and rely on their sisterwives or other women to care for their children; borrow and trade with other women who have more resources; build up an in-house industry, such as beekeeping, gardening, massage therapy, herbalism, or midwifery, which makes an excellent bargaining chip in the female network; bring in goods from outside family; rely on income and domestic help from their older children; or scrounge or steal goods from stores, government service offices, and others' homes and gardens.[6]

Meeting Economic Challenges

Judith

Thirty-six-year-old Judith Harris is a tiny, dark-haired, Hispanic woman who is the third wife of one of the most powerful men in the Allred group, a man who supervises and sanctions plural marriages and oversees the Harker community budget and financial stewardships. This man is constantly traveling to and from Salt Lake City to participate in council meetings, and, when in Harker, he has a demanding construction job that keeps him away from home. Furthermore, Judith's husband has three other wives (one wife died) and approximately 50 children, and he visits his wives on a rotation basis that allows fewer than 8 days on average per monthly visit with Judith's family. In order to provide for his wives and many children, he often leaves the budgeting of expenses to each wife and expects them to engage in creative financing to get through each month.[7]

In 1989, my daughter and I lived with Judith for several weeks and visited her after that on an irregular basis. I observed that she used a family budget sheet to keep track of any income and expenses that she incurred during the month in caring for her five children and her co-wife's two children, who were under her care temporarily (figure 8). Judith categorized all her monthly expenses: tithing, clothing, food, recreation, gifts, necessary items, miscellaneous items, and family. Incredibly, her expenses from October 17 to November 30 totaled barely $76. This amount is her portion of her husband's salary. Her expenses vary from postage stamps to cough drops, but on the whole, they are items that involve children, school, or recreation. Much of Judith's staple foods and many of her household items came from *other* sources.

Judith, her co-wives, and a few other women, including Judith's sister, Kay, combine efforts in building up their winter stores. Each woman tends a garden, and together they get fruit from orchards and family outside the group, all of which they preserve for storage by canning and freezing. The "winter staple storage," as it is called, provides enough food for all their families through the winter and most of the spring. Each woman's contribution to the storage is recorded so that her withdrawal from it does not exceed the limit. Judith works closely with her birth sister, Kay; other women in charge of key staples like honey, milk, and eggs; and her co-wives, Milly, Sherrie, and Barbara, who provided her with most of the other necessities. Through the informal yet efficient system of the Harker grapevine, Judith is able to find any spare items that she needs, such as used appliances, washers, brooms, mops, can openers, girls' dresses, boys' socks, a spool of thread, maple extract, or some yarrow tea for a child's cold. The female economic network is not based on a balanced reciprocity; on the contrary, I would call it unbalanced for several reasons. There is no immediate expectation that a gift will be returned, and it may take weeks, months, and even years before someone returns a favor with a payment in kind.

Because Judith's income is extremely limited, her food budget relies on wheat that is ground by the communal mill, brown rice purchased in bulk quantities by certain female friends, communal honey raised by the mayor's first wife, and milk that is distributed at a discount price by her neighbors. She has quite a few shelves of canned fruit from the winter

ITEM	INCOME	EXPENSE	BALANCE	TITHING	CLOTH.	FOOD	REC.	GIFTS	NECES.	MISC.	FAM.
cash	12.54		12.54								
baby-sitting	3.25	0.25	15.54	0.25							
tithing		0.33	15.21	0.33						0.25	
stamps		0.25	14.96								
baby-sitting	8.00		22.96								
tithing		0.80	22.16								
baby-sitting	26.00		48.16							0.25	
tithing		2.60	45.56	2.60							
red ribbon		0.25	45.31								
insurance		19.00	26.31						19.00		
library fine		0.02	26.29							0.02	
picture reprints		0.65	25.64							0.65	
picture payback	0.65		26.29								
chips, zingers		1.28	25.01			1.28					
apple juice		0.50	24.51			0.50					
school play		1.00	23.51				1.00				
school pictures		14.00	9.51						14.00		
treasure of truth		2.50	7.01						2.50		
baby-sitting	2.00		9.01								
tithing		0.20	8.81	0.20							
baby-sitting	3.00		11.81								
tithing		0.30	11.51	0.30							
hamburger	1.24	1.24	11.51			1.24					
pantyhose		2.00	9.51		2.00						
baby-sitting	2.08		11.59								
tithing		0.28	11.31	0.28							
men's cologne		1.78	9.53					1.78			
bracelet		2.97	6.56					2.97			
orange juice		0.65	5.91			0.65					
hamburger		3.00	2.91			3.00					
drink		0.35	2.56			0.35					
fries		1.68	0.88			1.68					
drink payback	0.05		0.93								
grape juice/pie		1.68	-0.75			1.68					
speech payment	3.00	3.00	-0.75						3.00		
primary show		0.22	-0.97				0.22				
cough drops	0.40	0.40	-0.97							0.40	
baby-sitting	3.00		2.03								
tithing		0.30	1.73	0.30							
kitchen towel		0.70	1.03							0.70	
choc. cherry		0.69	0.34					0.69			
shoes	10.00	10.00	0.34		10.00						
TOTALS	75.21	74.87	0.34	4.26	12.00	10.38	1.22	5.44	38.50	2.27	

Figure 8. This budget represents the earnings and expenses of one polygynist wife, the third wife of a Harker councilman. It is typical of many Harker wives' budgets, which are shown to their husbands and, later, to their bishops to account for monthly spending activities.

staple stores and various other foodstuffs purchased in bulk. She also relies, although somewhat infrequently, on beef products purchased from the community herd at discount. Judith's wood is gathered locally or purchased at a low, bulk rate. The wood for most of the community is usually delivered by a large truck to various woodsheds throughout the community and purchased through a local sawmill that sells remnant pieces cheaply. Judith and her friends also go regularly to spring and summer rummage sales in the larger towns of the area, where they find all kinds of household "treasures" for very little money.

Overall, I would say Judith was the most enterprising, intelligent woman of my study. I admired the way she operated her household, like a battleship, with a strict division of labor and a dedicated group of children who obeyed her every word. The food was nutritious, albeit not abundant. We ate wheat bread, canned fruit, and homemade butter and cheese. We had plenty of eggs and milk, which were delivered through the communal network. All in all, it was a spartan lifestyle for me—I lost 15 pounds while there—and extremely inexpensive. Judith could write a book on creative household management and make quite a bit of money doing so. Her children were by and large healthy, active, and productive—no one went without. And with the help of her co-wives, Judith was able to spend time in the school library, where she catalogued papers and books. Her life was full but not exhaustive. She seems quite content and satisfied in her home and with her husband, although she did not see him very often.

When I asked her about all of the materials and necessities that she needed to satisfy the needs of comfort, she said simply, "Janet, you have to realize that when you remove the desire and expectation of certain creature comforts, you don't miss them when they aren't around." To my knowledge, at the time of the writing of this book, Judith is still in her duplex, with only three of her children at home. When all of her children are gone, she will likely move into her sister's home and give her duplex to some new wife or recent convert.

April

April is a 25-year-old mother of four young children and the third wife of a computer software salesman. She came into the group last year with three children, a penniless widow from Salt Lake City. She had a history of emotional illness, and was a victim of sex abuse as a child. She met and married a man with two other wives who inspired her to join the polygynous group. She believes in him and his righteousness but wishes that he could provide her with a better place to live.

At present, she lives in a tiny trailer on the east side of town and has a budget of less than $50 per month. She complains that her children are the first ones in the whole town to contract illnesses, and she is the last one to receive aid. She says that she did not immunize her children because she did not want to go into town and be seen by the other women and be asked questions about her relationship to her husband. She also spoke about the high cost of health care "on the outside" and said that the Lord would provide her children with what they needed.

She does not get along with her first sisterwife, who lives in a ranch-style home 4 miles from her and disapproves of April's belief in Eastern herbal medicine. Her other co-wife is pleasant enough, she said, but has seven children of her own and is struggling with economic troubles, too. She has two birth sisters also converted to the Work, but they are just as poverty-stricken as she is and live some distance from her; one is 10 miles away in another town, and the other lives in Salt Lake City.

Last winter, when the temperature dropped to 30 degrees below zero and her supply of winter garden storage was depleted, she borrowed the car from her first sisterwife, left her children with her birth sister, and went into town to get some food supplies. She needed oranges for her children's colds, some vitamins, and perhaps canned vegetables, but she only had $5 in her purse. She had spent quite a bit on her daughter's school clothes the previous week and was hoping for a check from her husband this week to make ends meet. Although he usually sends her money every 2 weeks, this week the family had to make do with less because all funds were going for one of the first wife's son's college expenses. The $5 was all she had in the world.

Once in the supermarket, April paid for a gallon of milk and several cans of corn and beans. She took them to the car and just sat there for nearly an hour, wondering how she was going to get the oranges and vitamins. Determined, she walked into the store and went over to the pharmacy section, reached down, and slipped a plastic bottle of herbal multiple vitamins in her pocket. She then asked one of the bagboys to help her with her box of oranges that she had bought. She pointed to the one she wanted, and the young man carried it to her car without asking questions.

"I drove like a bat out of hell. I couldn't believe I had just stolen a box of oranges," she said, crying bitterly at the memory of it. Once back in Harker, she went to her birth sister's house to pick up her children and gave her a few of the precious oranges. She then went to her second co-wife and gave her some of the oranges. "How did you afford these oranges?" she asked, knowing that April had no money.

April told her that she managed to take them out of the store without paying for them. Her sisterwife then repeated a popular Allredite tenet, "The Lord understands it when we find creative ways of getting by—if that means stealing from the Gentiles, then that is what we have to do."

This last Christmas, April was faced with preparing a dinner of olives and lettuce for her children, when there was a ring of the doorbell. When she opened the door, she saw a beautiful fat turkey and $100 attached to

it. She is not positive where the donation came from. She believes it was
from her "guardian angel," she said. She later says it was from a Harker
woman who is always looking out for her.

April says that she has experienced many such ups and downs in her
stay in Harker. It seems that just when she is ready to give it all up,
something wonderful happens, and an angel sends food and goods to her.
Her approach to survival is on a day-to-day basis, with very little thought
to beyond a week or a year. Rather than involve herself with the networking at which Judith is such an expert, April is unsure of her place
with the other women and is afraid to ask the councilmen for help. It
would mean that her husband was unfit to care for her. "He would be
reprimanded and made fun of," she said. "He is a good man, and I know
that he would care for me if he could."

April is considering going on welfare for the next few months, until
her husband's computer business gets off the ground. She has heard from
other women in Harker that the government will give out generous
monthly payments for women who can prove that their husbands have
neglected them.

"That's easy enough for me," said April, "because I'm not legally
married to my husband. In fact, I still use my maiden name so I won't be
arrested or so that people won't put me down." Her motives for refusing
to join the network were unclear to me, but her drive to survive was
inspiring. I had no doubt that she would achieve her goals of gaining
welfare. I did not hear about her success in that area when I returned on
my second visit. When I asked her husband about her financial situation,
he seemed embarrassed and changed the subject. It is considered dishon-
orable for women to go on welfare and, of course, shoplifting is a "sin."

Gretchen

Gretchen is 35 years old and the first wife of a man who owns a small
business in another state, where he lives with his third wife. She has five
children, and her sisterwife, Susan, has three. They all live in the same
split-level house on the outskirts of town. She said she enjoys her sisterwife's companionship and cooperation. They rotate meals and housclean-
ing every other day. Sometimes, they rotate by week for variety, or when
something comes up, such as postpartum depression. On nights when
Gretchen is free, she spends time with other friends, goes to a movie, or
just reads at home.

"On the night I must cook, I feel like cooking. I feel refreshed and
ready to do a good job," she said.

Once a week, Gretchen and Susan sit down and do the budgeting of their husband's income from the store and their own meager incomes from teaching school.

> We have x number of dollars for cooking, x for clothing, etc. We make a menu plan for the month and prepare a grocery list. Since Susan likes to stay at home and I am a goer, I do the shopping, while she watches the kids. We structure our lives and our children and the house together. It's easier that way. We vary home maintenance to fit our immediate needs. For example, a while ago I taught first grade till noon in language and reading. We both had young infants, and so Susan did light housekeeping during those hours. Then we would eat at noon together, and she would teach my same first-grade class social studies and math from 1:00 to 3:30 while I tended and did cooking for dinner. We both were able to give the time and care our young babies needed.

One year, however, Susan got very sick with the pregnancy of her last child and had to remain in bed for several months. Gretchen's support system was suddenly halted. For a few weeks, she said, everything went fine. They ate their storage goods and kept spending down to a minimum. But Gretchen was finding it hard to teach, clean the house, take care of the kids, and do the cooking for everyone, so she quit her job teaching. As a result, the family began suffering for want of food and necessities. Their husband, Paul, did not make enough money to *lend* to Gretchen and Susan until the birth of Susan's baby. In many polygynist households, men often see any money contributed above the bare essentials as a loan to their wives.

So Gretchen went to the social services office in the nearby town and requested welfare. She told them that her husband had left her with eight "illegitimate" kids and she was destitute. The office gave her $700 per month, not including food stamps, more than enough to see her co-wife and herself through the next few months, until social services discontinued the payments. "When it comes to feeding and caring for your children, you can't be too proud," Gretchen said. "You take what you can get . . . what you desperately need."

Although I never interviewed anyone from social services, I had the feeling that many women are able to gain the funds they need because of their appearance and their number of children. It is also helpful that the Bitterroot Valley is going through a widespread recession, so that the polygynous women are not singled out as the only recipients of welfare. The manner in which Gretchen was able to secure welfare is typical, I was told, of many women who go through periods of poverty. Once they are able to get back on their feet, they then discontinue the welfare checks, and things will be much the same as they were before, with rotation schedules and shared incomes. There are some families, however, who never get off welfare.

I was told the story of Brother Bart, who married eight women and lived in a 5,000-square-foot cabin in the center of Harker. Brother Bart was a retired military officer who spent his time writing pamphlets and manuals on government conspiracy and survival. All of his wives were on welfare, I was told. His eldest wife was recovering from a kidney operation. When I asked how much it cost the family, I was told that it was covered by Medicaid.

THE LIVES OF THESE THREE WOMEN raise many significant questions about the nature of women's role in society. Women *do* contribute importantly to their subsistence, and women have a variety of ways of surviving in a poverty-stricken area. Husbands are usually a source of support, but more often than not women rely on a network of other women for a major source of their material needs for themselves and their families.

five

*

Courtship, Marriage, and Sexuality

Most Allred women are able to use polygyny to their advantage. The following stories generally confirm that female converts are upwardly mobile in their progression to marry well and find a relatively comfortable home for themselves and their children. This chapter describes the socialization, courtship, and marriage rules and norms not already mentioned in chapter 2. It then provides several narratives of women's experience in marriage that illustrate the broad range of experiences of both convert and established wives. Finally, drawing upon community demographic statistics on marriage and family, it shows how convert women and elite established men have advantages over convert males in the kingdom-building process.

Socialization

Harker socialization produces a psychological and sociological conformity that marks the community as a distinct religious group and makes it difficult for people to either enter or exit the group. This conformity makes it hard for members to blend into the larger Gentile world. For example, the community's members attempt to dress in popular clothing, but they seem to stand out in the modest and inexpensive way they dress. Women are often seen with hair longer than usual and a small, outward "sausage curl" on the top of the forehead. They wear dresses or pants under the dresses, with the hem below the knee by at least 4 inches. Men dress in a rural, fashion, with bill caps and country jackets. They are sometimes seen in town with one middle-aged woman and one younger woman, as if a married couple were taking their baby-sitter on an outing. Harker

80

children are recognized by their high school teachers by their striking resemblance to each other, their dress their same last names, and their tendency to group themselves together. In general, Harker residents are extremely secretive and nonsocial to outsiders, keeping the expressive aspects of their lives limited to the confines of their homes, church, and community.

Further, Harker socialization functions to perpetuate religious belief and community commitment. It is a consistent, continuous process, building up to three peaks in the life of the individual: *baptism*, or membership into the sect; *marriage*, or the "everlasting covenant" with God; and *death*, or entrance into the kingdom of heaven. The pattern of socialization is remarkably consistent throughout the community; deviance is rare but does occur in the adolescent stages, mostly among males.[1]

Birth and Infancy

Among many members, the perception is that the more children born to a woman, the more blessed she will be. I was told that people live by the maxim "We don't believe in birth control; we believe in self-control." Formal methods of birth control are not allowed.[2] Sexual activity during lactation, pregnancy, or menstruation is explicitly forbidden. Children are raised primarily in extended families—made up of nuclear units of each wife and her children—and are brought into the community school system at the age of 2 or 3, depending on the parents.

School training involves Montessori instruction at ages 2 and 3, kindergarten at ages 4 and 5, and first through sixth grade, ages 6 through 12. A small group of junior high students are taught in the community, but after grade school, most children are bused to a Gentile school in "Jackson," 12 miles to the east.

Children of polygynous marriages are promised to be the strongest, most intelligent children of all God's kingdom (Allred 1984).[3] In spite of this, there is no formal recognition of a pregnancy by the community. When a woman finds out that she is pregnant, there is merely an informal recognition among the women that "so-and-so's" time has come and she will be needing their help. It is uncommon for husbands to modify their routines to help when any of their wives are pregnant. With approximately 40 to 50 children born per year, pregnancies are too frequent for the community to take special notice. One man with three or four wives averages 18 to 32 children. In light of these statistics, men would be altering their actions constantly if they were to aid their wives during confinement.

Religious training begins about age 2, when a mother folds a baby's arms and asks it to bow its head to pray with the others for the meal. This prayer training occurs at morning, bedtime, and mealtimes. Religion for the young child early on becomes a ritual, often associated with food, as a child learns automatically to fold its arms and bow its head when hungry and at the instant anyone calls for a prayer, at church or at home. Along with prayers, songs are taught early to young children, at home, at nursery, at Sunday school, and in Primary School. The mother begins teaching these songs to her baby while rocking it to sleep and continues to sing them to the child during work or play. These primary songs are basically hymn-type ditties for children about the Savior and his love for children, such as "Jesus Loves Me, This I Know," "Jesus Once Was a Little Child," and "I Am a Child of God." By the age of 3, the child is able to sing a few songs and pray alone.

Childhood

In raising young children, sex differentiation tasks are strictly enforced. The rules of conduct supported by the male ideological structure provide guidelines for this sex typing of children. The Harker United Order suggests that if any youth or child does forget the rules of conduct, the parents have to compensate for this disobedience in some way.

> If any child shall get beyond the control of parental direction and shall violate the rights or destroy, injure, or otherwise abuse or misuse the property of others, the parents shall be held responsible and shall compensate the Order or the individuals concerned for said destruction. (United Order doc., Cannon 1990, Appendix C, Article XI:2)

Harker girls work inside at cooking, cleaning, and sewing and outside at food-producing tasks such as tending gardens and canning fruit. Daughters help their mothers with washing, ironing, and other chores, training to be future wives and mothers. Ideas about professional careers are uncommon, but ideas about jobs and making money to support the family are routine. Ideally, fathers, in turn, reinforce gender differentiation in boys through exposure to masculine tasks and activities, but this training occurs with only a few of the sons, as there are so many. One woman told me her husband takes only the first wife's oldest boys fishing and hunting or to work in the toolshed after work. Boys' chores include caring for cattle, carrying firewood, moving machinery, and, in some cases, babysitting. They develop an early skill for mechanical and carpentry work by watching their fathers install a kitchen cabinet in a newly built home, repair the valves on a water box, or run the sawmill. But these jobs are eventually taken up by older men, and young men must go outside the branch to find employment.

In general, the socialization of children is left to the women and their older children. The training of children is complicated by the fact of parallel families living under the same father. Children of less favored wives or first (legal) wives are often treated differentially and given the message that they have no rights to the power of the Priesthood and so on. Therefore, children in most cases have much stronger ties to their mothers than to their fathers (Cannon 1990, Young 1954:241). A father is less likely to be around, and his influence is often just a threat floating on the air, broken by periodic desertion or even by death or divorce.

For a husband with three or four wives, which is the community average, and seven children per wife, there is little father–individual child time alloted in his busy schedule. Often a father comes home exhausted from work, seeking quiet refuge, and finds a house full of kids with Daddy on their minds. He may seek a quiet conversation with his wife, rather than discuss all of his children's problems and activities in the first 5 minutes. Some children get more regulating and instruction than others. For example, when a man visits his first wife's children, he knows them better, they are older, and he expects more of them. When he visits a second wife's children, some of whom may have been born to the woman's dead husband or to a man she divorced, he may be restrained in disciplining and bestowing spontaneous affection.[4] To children, fathers are always busy with one thing or another. Frequently, when it is Daddy's special night home and all are sitting around the table, he is suddenly called away to bless so-and-so, or help with some community priesthood problem or project.

At 5, children are expected to be obedient and begin to learn how to behave as they should in conforming to the rituals of the church and community. They say their prayers, clean their rooms, and complete their chores. They must learn to be quiet in church; they must sit still and be attentive to the sermon. At 6, they must begin to familiarize themselves with the group's scriptural canon, which includes the King James Bible, the *Doctrine and Covenants*, the *Pearl of Great Price*, the *Book of Mormon*, and the *Journal of Discourses*, as well as other early Mormon church doctrinal writings.

During grade school, children are counseled to take the knowledge and talents they have been given by God and, ideally, use them to benefit the community and their families. They are encouraged to run errands and to work on their own. Any money they earn is handed over to their father, who then hands it over to the bishop. Most of the child's day is spent under close supervision by someone in authority—teachers, principal, or a parent. Some children do not attend school but, rather, stay home and baby-sit their younger brothers and sisters so their mothers can work. One boy of 9 had the task of caring for his six younger siblings from 7 A.M. to 6 P.M. while his mother worked in the nearby town. A girl of 11 had seven siblings to care for.

For those who attend school, much time is spent playing during several recess sessions, where they are, for the most part, allowed to do as they wish. It is through watching children at play that the inequalities in socialization patterns become apparent. On one occasion, in a fight between two boys over a ball, the bigger boy grabbed the ball from the smaller boy. The smaller boy was crying, but nothing was done for him, though an instructor watched the whole thing. When asked about the crisis, she said that the bigger child was a Harris, one of the "named" (high-ranking established) families; the other child was a Johnson, a lower ranked family. Once she had tried to bring a fight to the attention of the principal, who was a Harris, and he laughed at her and said, "That's just the pecking order; there's nothing we can do." Another woman told me that her son was always being hit with arrowguns or splat balls on his way home from school by boys of high-ranking families. Furthermore, I was told that many children do not have the same opportunity for advancement in the school system and that it favors established family offspring.[5]

Peer pressure among age sets is an effective tool for propagating the laws of the Work. By exploiting the desire for acceptance, doubts about the Work's practices are overcome by offering a sense of belonging to an affirming community. Believing is a high status marker among children ages 7 or 8, as they prepare for baptism, which marks their official entrance into the group. At this age, children are taught unquestioning obedience to fundamentalist authority. Children try to please by memorizing scriptures, doing well in school, singing loudly, and obeying their parents, thus furthering themselves in the system of achievement. Often, young children of 8 to 12 are asked to come up to the pulpit in front of all the community on Sunday to say a few words about their "testimony" in the form of an extemporaneous speech. This practice keeps children prepared spiritually and makes them conscientious about the group's activities. Also, like many other rural communities, the belt strap is used to enforce discipline. This form of punishment is used often on boys, who "more than the girls must learn what it takes to live the 'fullness.' " (I remark later in the book how this punishment may contribute to the large numbers of young men who later leave the group.)[6] At age 8, children go through their second religious ritual, baptism. (Prayer is considered the first religious ritual.) They are examined by the bishop beforehand to assess that they have been taught about the grave responsibility they are taking on, and then a spot is chosen, usually Sam's pond, and children are taken, dressed in white, to walk into the water with their father or another member of the priesthood. They are immersed completely for a few seconds and then taken out of the water. The priesthood bearer who officiates, usually a child's father, bestows the baptism ordinance by the power of the priesthood, in the "name of the Father, and of the Son, and of the Holy Ghost." Baptism is the same as in the LDS Church.

At 12, children are again interviewed by the bishop and during this meeting recite several scriptures chosen for each. They also recite "The Articles of Faith" translated by Joseph Smith from the *Pearl of Great Price*. These basic tenets of the Mormon Church are utilized by the Harker community as guides throughout their lives and are often repeated during sermons as reminders of how they should structure their belief system. After passing the bishop's interview, the 12-year-olds then leave primary school (as they do in the Mormon church) and enter the young men's and young women's organizations. No longer children, girls are expected to further develop the skills necessary for motherhood and polish their talents in the home. Boys are ordained "deacons" in the Aaronic priesthood and begin to climb up the steps of the male authority structure by setting up for the sacrament and helping all other priesthood members.[7]

Youth

It is in the young women's and priesthood or Boy Scout organizations that the girls and boys begin to separate themselves fully by gender, and the male-female subcultures are further distinguished. Now the young men are taught responsibility and a separateness from women through a mind-set that requires men to watch over women. The young women are taught to be strong in testimony, to learn skills that will help them in marriage, to be excellent mothers, and to distinguish and separate themselves from the authority structure of the community. (Boys at this same age are learning to identify themselves with this same structure.) Young women and men have increased responsibility at home and increased adult supervision and scrutiny, for this is the beginning of the courting years. During this transitional stage from childhood to adulthood, the community recognizes the physical and emotional changes of their youth and utilizes these changes to "build testimonies" in the youth.[8] "A testimony is the most important possession a person has," one young women told me. "It is faith in the Lord Jesus Christ and in his teachings." With a strong testimony, the youth are taught that they can move mountains. In spite of this great promise, adolescence is a time of emotional vacillation, when the loyalties of the individual have not completely crystallized. Disregard of community rules and mores is tolerated during this period.

Because adolescents are considered physically capable of a higher level of work, they are quickly incorporated into the community and family work structure and often get jobs outside to boost the family income. Pressure is especially keen on young men to find work and give their incomes to their fathers; however, I was surprised by the number of young women who also work outside the home.

In many of the interviews, I observed parents rationalize that their older children do not have much time between school, church, and work to be moody or skeptical or to question their teachings. In reality, at least in many of the families I visited, I noticed that while young women experienced a dualistic relationship with their mothers based on authority and tolerance and on love and friendship, between young men and their fathers there was only one: authority and punishment. Of the seven families I interviewed on my first visit to Harker, three experienced the loss of at least one male member through "apostasy" (although one of those left the Work to be baptized into the mainstream church), and two left the community in search of continued education and jobs. This is also true of the Short Creek (also known as Colorado City) fundamentalist community (Bradley 1990).

One theory that provides some explanation for why so many young men, rather than young women, leave the community is given by Seymour Parker and colleagues (1975), who studied father absence and cross-sex identity in the Short Creek fundamentalist group. They reexamined the puberty rites associated with John Whiting's studies and applied them to the polygynous society. They suggested that the absence of a father in a masculine-oriented milieu could result in a sex identity that causes conflict between father and son. Although they did not find a definitive cross-sex identity—that is, the boys did not want to be like their mothers—their study sheds light on how boys are affected by the "low salience of father" (1975:700). One young Harker man told me that he had succeeded in "breaking into the ranks" as a young man by being pals with one of the boys of the high-ranking family. They used to run around together, and he would get privileges that other boys did not get. Even so, the young man said, they were "all afraid of the Priesthood getting them." They were told that the high-ranking members could read minds and that they would *know* who was the perpetrator of a crime immediately. Many Harker young men turn to drugs and alcohol to cope with the pressures of their situations, which, in addition to tea and tobacco, are strictly forbidden. Very few families were unfamiliar with stories about young men who had an addiction of some sort or other, whether that be the need to hunt animals, drink alcohol, or "get into trouble." I argue that because of the widespread problem with young men, focus is placed on the first and second sons or favorites of families—those who have a "healthy" relationship with their fathers—who will be required to perpetuate plural marriage in the future. What this means, in effect, is that younger or nonfavorite sons are more or less abandoned by their busy polygynist fathers. They will not be encouraged to remain in the group as they are in direct competition for the valuable community resources with their own fathers and brothers, as well as all the other men.

Girls, by contrast, are given some degree of latitude in their socialization prior to marriage, if their parents can afford it. They are closely tied to the activities of their mothers yet not restricted to them. Many of them become active in local high school sports, drama, or other extracurricular clubs and remain active in the religious aspects of the community as well. Girls are taught in the "young women's program" the traditional skills of stitchery, embroidery, and sewing and often make their own dresses.

Courtship

Early in their teens, girls work to build their trousseaus and rarely challenge their imminent position as polygynist wives.[9] In the larger group, the priesthood head counsels girls to wait until they are at least 18 years old before marrying, although there is still a high rate of 16-and 17-year-old marriages. In the Harker branch, there is not such an emphasis, and young women may marry as young as 14 or 15 if it is sanctioned by the council.

One-on-one dating among the young people is not encouraged, however, and it is more common to see groups of young people together—skating on the pond, working on a project, or talking outside church after a meeting—than a young couple doing those same activities. There is very little difference in this light between Harker and Mormonism in general. Some are vague about how to date in the first place. For example, one young man went on a date with a girl and was strictly reprimanded and told that the proper procedure is to telephone her father and ask permission for a date, and then the date will be scheduled.

It is not uncommon, however, for an older man, from age 40 to 80, to date a teenage girl, with the permission of her father and the matchmaker.[10]

In some cases, "appointed" men in "good standing" can give permission for others to court; that is, those ordained by the councilmen to perform special functions may do so without restraint. This practice is often considered a check against the libido of men in general, but, in reality, it is a device the priesthood hierarchy uses to control the distribution of wives.

By requesting a dance at the town social or by inviting her out with his family for a picnic, a man is showing interest in a woman as a possible mate. Ideally, before any courting of this sort occurs, the man is advised by the matchmaker, who speaks to the woman's father about it. Yet, many times, the natural attraction between a man and a woman leads to ignoring some of the lines of authority and proceeds without an advising third party. At times, the third party is the suitor's wife, who may encourage him to court one woman rather than another.

Besides courtship, proper dress and conduct are the main concerns of Harker young women. Clothing, jewelry, and makeup for vanity's sake are frowned on in most families, especially tight clothing, flashy colors, or any fashion that emphasizes the human anatomy. Low necklines, sleevelessness, and shorts for women are considered unseemly and immodest. For some, even cutting of the hair, coloring of the hair, or excessive jewelry is not allowed. Many times, the following scripture is read to young women at their meeting to remind them not to forget their appearances: "Because the daughters of Zion are haughty and walk with stretched-forth necks and wanton eyes, walking and mincing as they go, and making a tinkling with their feet . . . (Isaiah 3:16). About age 16, an age of accountability for both sexes, young members of Harker are taken to a General Priesthood Council member for a "patriarchal blessing." This blessing provides a map or blueprint for life, if they remain true to the faith. It also reveals their true heritage as sons and daughters of the Tribes of Israel, stating which tribes they stem from. The blessing is personalized by the patriarch who gives the ordinance, and the youths are told what to avoid and what to look for in life."[11]

Marriage

Polygynous wives, both convert and established, enjoy many advantages in the system. Of particular interest is the presence of hypergamy and sister-wife kinship, both of which strengthen women's position in the group.

Hypergamy

Harker women are bound by a commandment (Young 1861) that, if for any reason they are not satisfied with their course of salvation with the present husband, they are obliged to marry a higher ranked priesthood bearer. In the mainstream Mormon Church, this rule is not required.

Given this general rule of hypergamy, the selection of a wealthier, more prestigious man as a second husband after the first one died would be the ideal. A woman's second husband is a temporal consort, not necessarily as diligent in faith but a good provider. In the second marriage, the desire for comfort is stronger. For unmarried women, polygyny allows salvation through a postmortem nuptial ceremony—that is, a type of "ghost marriage" after death for those who could not find their mates on earth. Some older women, often mothers or sisters, are married for socioreligious reasons—that is, solely for the salvation they will receive. To reach the highest kingdom, a person must be married, just as Christ is married.

Another advantage women have in the system is the ease with which they can be released from an unsatisfying marriage contract, which allows more of them to marry upward. Divorce here is defined the dissolution of a spiritual and social contract that is not necessarily based on civil laws. For example, a woman coming into the group may already be legally married to a man outside the group. It is her new marriage to a member of the group that is observed, and this new "holy" contract is considered the real contract. Divorce is often called "gaining a release" in the group, which suggests the ease with which individuals can break their contracts. Overall, women are able to gain releases from their husbands with greater ease than men are able to do so.

The divorce rate in 1992 was approximately 35% of all marriages transacted, based on the statistics announced in a priesthood session that spring.[12] About 40% of marriages ended in release, divorce, or abandonment. Men who are unhappy with their wives have a harder time in gaining releases from them. The official rule in the Allred group is that men are obliged to care for women to whom they become sealed for all eternity. This bond cannot easily break unless the man can show that the woman is bewitched, a Babylonian (a paganistic, worldly, non-Gentile), or that she is abusive to her children. Very few male-requested releases have been granted, according to a 1993 sermon in Harker. Women have a much stronger obligation to find the right man to take them and their children to the kingdom of God. Therefore, council members are more sympathetic to women who desire better men than to men who desire better women. "There are plenty of righteous women to go around," explained one council member.

Propinquity and congeniality between wives play a large role in the courtship process. One wife who was barren began courting a young woman and then suggested to her husband that he marry her. Yet, social mobility is an obvious factor, too. Another woman admitted that she married her husband not for his good looks or sex appeal but because he was tied closely to a council member's family and was considered one of their "appointees." As one woman said, "Any girl would have taken a successful Bishop though he be married, in preference to a single man with nothing" (Young 1954:120).

Women of Harker use their position as wives to their advantage in negotiating resources. They also use their close kinship with other women, both convert and established, to form opposing forces to their husbands and other men of the community. Of the many diverse tools women use to manipulate their relative status vis-à-vis men, kinship among sisterwives is the most useful.

Kinship among Sisterwives

It is not uncommon for women to be related to their sisterwives even before marrying into a family as sisters, cousins, aunts and nieces, sisters-in-laws, or affines. Because of this, their bonds are more tightly woven than if they were married as strangers into their husband's kin group. An illustration of the close kin ties women share with their own sisterwives and with other women of the community is found in the table in figure 9. To show how families are intertwined through kinship and marriage, I have drawn up a small genealogy of the common ancestor of several Harker residents, Joseph L. Harris (figure 10).

For the Harris and Olson families, who intermarry frequently, kinship association is somewhat confusing. Beth Harris's children are some of Mary Olson's children's closest friends as well as their cousins and aunts and uncles, simultaneously. Because Beth and Mary are natural sisters as well as sisterwives, their children have become cousins to each other yet at the same time are brothers and sisters through their father. Because some of the older children's offspring are the same age as their brothers and sisters, these children have become aunts and uncles.

The genealogy of Joseph L. Harris's family, as well as the Harris-Olson example of intermarriage, illustrates certain marriage patterns among these polygynous communities. I derived further information on these patterns from interviews and additional genealogical research. I observed patterns of men who married sisters, brothers who married sisters, and cousins who married two separate sets of cousins. Sororal polygyny is by far the most common form of consanguineous marriage. The marriage of cousins to the same man is the second most common form. For example, in Harker, Melvin and Matt Harris married Judith, Jean, and Deborah Hanson. Rulon

FATHER	MOTHER	EGO	SPOUSE	COWIVES	RELATION TO SPOUSE	RELATION TO COWIFE
JLJ	MP	BOB	SUE	JANE		SISTER
J	UJ	NAN	RAY	DEB		NIECE/AUNT
JLJ	BA	KEN	ANN	SARA		AUNT/NIECE
JLJ	WP	LARRY	LIZ		COUSIN	
JLJ	MP	MARK	JAN	LYNN		SISTER
MK	CA	EMMA	JERRY	SUE,JO, EVA, RA		COUSIN
JLJ	BA	EVA	JERRY	RA, JO, SUE, EMMA		SISTER
JLJ	BA	RA	JERRY	SUE, JO,EVA, EMMA		SIS, COUSIN
JLJ	BA	JO	JERRY	RA, EVA, SUE, EMMA		SIS, COUSIN
JLJ	BA	SUE	JERRY	RA, JO, EVA, EMMA		SIS, COUSIN
JLJ	WP	FAY	BOB	JANE		SISTER
JLJ	WP	JANE	BOB	FAY		SISTER
JLJ	BA	TOM	LOUISE	VERA, NEL, DEB,	COUSIN	SIS, NIECE, COUSIN
MA	KJ	TOM	DEB	NEL, VERA, LOU	COUSIN	SIS, AUNT, COUSIN
MA	KJ	TOM	NEL	DEB, VERA, LOU	COUSIN	SIS, AUNT, COUSIN
JLJ	BA	TOM	VERA	LOU, NEL,DEB	COUSIN	SIS, NIECE, COUSIN
JLJ	MP	DON	BARB		COUSIN	
O	MP	CARI	LOU	JO, SUE		1/2 SIS, 1/2 AUNT
JLJ	WP	ELSE	MARK	BARB, SAR	SISTER	
JLJ	WP	SARA	MARK	BARB, ELSE	SISTER	
JLJ	WP	BARB	MARK	ELSE, SAR	SISTER	
MA	JJ	KATH	MATT	DONNA	COUSIN	
JLJ	MP	MELV	SHEL	NAN		COUSIN
JLJ	MP	MARG	ROB	MEG		SISTER
JLJ	MP	MEG	ROB	MARG		SISTER
MA	EJ	SUE	BERT	CARI, SAR	SISTER	
MA	EJ	CARI	BERT	SUE, SARA		SISTER
MA	EJ	SARA	BERT	SUE, CARI		SISTER
JLJ	MP	NANC	ROY			
JLJ	MP	MIKE	CATH	JAN		SISTER
JLJ	MP	MELV	NAN	SHEL		COUSIN
JLJ	BA	JEAN	GEOR	ALICE		COUSIN
MA	KJ	LISA	TIM	MARY, LIZ		1/2 SIS
MA	EJ	LIZ	TIM	LISA, MAR	1/2 SIS	
MA	EJ	MARY	TIM	LIZ, LISA		1/2 SIS
HJ	E	BARB	TROY	LOU, ANN		1/2 COUS
M	L	LOU	TROY	ANN, BARB		1/2 COUS
MJ	N	ANN	TROY	BARB, LOU		1/2 COUS

Figure 9.   This chart shows the nature of relationships between co-wives, and between wives and their husbands. Note the significant number of sisters and cousins who marry the same man, intensifying the closeness of blood and marriage between women.

Allred, the former prophet, married Mary and Melba Clark. Mark, Rulon's brother, married three Harris sisters—Louise, Matilda, and Ruth—and Larry Harris married two Martin sisters, Carry and Elizabeth. Three Paterson boys married three Parson girls, and Tom Clark married his cousins Rachel and Kathy Peterson.

The significance of kinship among sisterwives is that women who live near their female relations reinforce each other and protect each other's interests, whether emotional, economic, or religious. The physical association with others—especially family—means living near people who believe the same way you do.

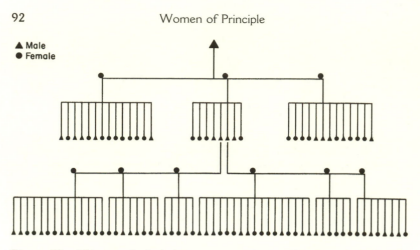

Figure 10. This genealogical chart represents the actual progeny of one Harker patriarch, his three wives, their 35 children, and the offspring of two sons who have each married three wives, and their 56 children. These two sons are a representation of the number of offspring that the other 35 children would have. The average number of children born to a male descendant, given this sample, is 28; the average number of children born to a female offspring is 7. Given these averages, it is estimated that the total number of grandchildren born to the Harker patriarch is 560.

In summary, socialization, courtship, and marital patterns promote female solidarity through common experiences in childbirth, religious conviction, motherhood, and homemaking. From birth to death, females are taught to work with each other to "build the kingdom" and to share all that they have with their co-wives. As toddlers, they learn to share toys and the attention of their mothers and fathers, and as grade school students they share testimonials and experience the peer pressure of religious conviction. As teens, they share in preparation for marriage and their future homes through the exchange of skills, stories, and spiritual support. And, in old age, they share in their preparation for death, when they will continue to relinquish part of their heavenly kingdom to their sisterwives. Polygynous wives are upwardly mobile, have a tight kinship network, and can be easily released (with some exceptions) from unsavory marital unions to better their economic and social position in society.

Miriam

Miriam is a beautiful, red-haired, slender 16-year-old who receives straight A's and is a member of the track team in the local high school. She is a native to polygyny, having grown up in a prominent established family in which four women shared one husband. She says she longs to marry a boy her own age and, in fact, has her sights set on Joe, an attractive high school senior who has a "cute smile." But Miriam is extremely practical about life. She says that life with Joe would be a temporary ride on the rollercoaster with very little bearing on the hereafter. She says that there are many advantages to marrying an older man who is "strong in his priesthoods." She looks forward to "rewarding sisterwife relationships" and is eager to be a mother and teach her children the gospel. She is currently being courted by two different men. One is Joe, a rather skinny, bare-faced, 18-year-old high school basketball player who converted to the group with his family last year. His family lives in the basement of another member's home until they can build their own home, which may take some time because his father is a salesclerk at an auto parts store. The other is a 55-year-old man who she claims has bad breath and hairy arms and whom she does not like. She is certain she will "straighten him out" at the soonest possible moment and let him know she has no interest.

She is fond of a 40-year-old man, a convert for 10 years, who has just built his two wives a beautiful home in the woods near the north creek, and she feels certain he returns her sentiments. His wives are "cool," she said, because they like the same things she does—a life in the woods, plenty of kids, and a lot of sharing. Besides, she would be able to have her own room in the new home, with a view of the town. She shares a room with two younger sisters in her present home.

She has not yet told her father or the town's matchmaker about her fondness for Ken, the 40-year-old, because she is also interested in continuing her education. She told me she will have to do a lot of praying and accept what "the Lord has in store for her." In the meantime, because of the informal group rule against marriages before 18, she will bide her time and enjoy the process.

"It is so different being courted by Harker men than it is when dating high school boys from the larger town," she said. "Here, every man, both young and old, is fair game. For men seeking women, it is harder because there are only so many women to choose from. I am lucky because I get my pick."

Betsy

Betsy, a 22-year-old second wife, mother of two children, recalls her courtship days when she, her husband-to-be, and his wife would go to the movies together as a threesome. She loved that type of courtship system because she was just as fond of her co-wife as she was of her husband. She said it was the period in her life when the three of them were the closest, and she longs for the time when they can get out together again.

As the fourth daughter of a prominent established family in Harker, she was interested in going to college and getting a degree before getting married. She had prospects for marriage but did not encourage any of them until she met Matt. He was different because of his persistence, his handsomeness, and his "appetite" for the gospel. She told him that she would wait a year while she attended college, and then she would let him know her decision. At the end of that year, she, Matt, and his first wife, Jill, began going out together on official dates. They went to the movies together. They ate at the 4-Bs restaurant on Friday nights. They even went camping over the Easter break.

"It seemed everyone had known all along that I would be a member of the family—it just fit. We went to dinner and walks together; we spend long hours into the night talking about doctrine and family," Betsy says.

Two months after the beginning of the official courtship, the three gathered with one of the councilmen in "a sacred spot" for the marriage ceremony and were sealed together for all eternity.

According to Betsy, the marriage ceremony can take place in a home, a church, a meadow, or on the top of a mountain, so long as it is performed by the proper priesthood authority.[14] One woman said she had been sealed to her husband in the company of one witness in a hidden room in a building "somewhere," in order to keep the marriage quiet.[15] For Betsy, it was performed on the "lookout"[16] hill west of town with a view of the Bitterroot Valley. Betsy told me that, typically, in the ceremony, the husband is presented with the new wife by the latest wife in the "patriarchal grip," a form of handshake that is sacred to the group as a symbol of the law of Sarah. In the Bible, Sarah gave Abraham her handmaiden, Hagar, to marry because Sarah herself was unable to bear children. It is the senior or latest wife who gives her husband the wife, though she may have no choice in whom her husband ultimately chooses to marry. It is a symbolic gesture of commitment to the bride and to the Principle. All the other wives, if present, may then place their hands on top of the wedding couple's clasp, and they are all sealed together for eternity. In this way, not only is the husband married to the bride but also each wife is married to her as well.

During the ceremony, which is the most important ordinance in the group, certain "oaths and covenants" are made. These oaths involve several promises to obey the laws of the gospel, to obey the law of consecration, or the United Order, to obey the law of chastity, and, for the wives, to obey their husbands and their God. The "sealing," the eternal bond between married persons, is an ordinance that calls on the "Holy Spirit of Promise" to assure that the sealings will be made for eternity.[17] The priesthood garment, which is a white, full-length undergarment that contains symbols of priesthood powers and covenants and reminders to walk in the straight and narrow path of righteousness, is often worn by those who have made the marital covenants. I was told that only those individuals who have entered the orthodox Mormon temples, such as those in Salt Lake City, Orem, or Provo, or those who have done their "sealing" work in the group's endowment house wear these special garments. Those who have not must wait until they are invited to do "ordinance" work in the endowment house before they are allowed to wear the garment.[18]

Betsy's description of the wedding ceremony should not be taken to be the general form of *all* Allred group marriages, for there are as many types of weddings as there are types of living arrangements and family sizes. One woman told me that she had 1 hour's notice for her wedding, and it was held in her apartment in the middle of the night. Another said she was not married with her co-wives present, nor did they know of her existence until 6 months after the wedding took place. Many weddings that took place during the John Ray years were secretive. Sometimes, it is a matter of protection from the law; otherwise, they would have been thrown in jail. For some couples, the ceremony was followed by an elaborate oration by the priesthood bearer in charge about the challenges plural marriage will bring; most ceremonies are less elaborate and comprised of the couple standing in front of the administrator with the other wives in a row from first to last. The administrator then asks the first wife if she gives her consent to the new wife, and he places each wife's hand in the bride's hand. Then the husband's hand is placed in the bride's hand, and the administrator marries them in the name of the Melchizedek Priesthood. As part of this ceremony, the adminstrator asks the couple—and the other wives who are present—to covenant obedience to various laws specified in the Mormon endowment ceremony, which, in effect, requires the women to obey their husband, as he obeys the Lord, as well as a number of other sacred commandments. Though all Allred group marriage ceremonies contain this same covenantal oration, the circumstances of the marriage vary. One couple I know was married without the presence of the man's other wives. Another couple married in the backseat of a car in transit to another state. Still another marriage had the full regalia of wives, white dresses, flowers, music, and family present. The secrecy with which many marriages occur reflects the former days of persecution and arrest, when plural wives were hidden away from the law.

After Betsy explained this ceremony to me, she remarked that she is truly glad to be a plural wife and feels that polygyny makes the total woman—a woman who can be anything she wants to be.

> In monogamy you are tied to a husband for economic sustenance, enter-tainment, conversation, comradeship, and emotional stimulation. But a po-lygynous wife is free and independent by necessity and makes her ties with other women. When a monogamous wife doesn't have him [the husband] around, and with no other sisterwives around, she is helpless. Where does she get the friendship, the moral support? A polygynist wife has it all.

Betsy further stated that she had some difficulty when her husband married a third wife, but it later passed and she learned to love and accept her new sisterwife. She said there are three steps that a polygynist wife goes through: (1) Initially, the husband is attracted to another woman, which is difficult because generally she is younger and sexually attractive to him and therefore could be rivals with you; (2) then, you learn to love her because you love him, and you want to make him happy; and (3) last, you realize that she (and her children, if relevant) deserve such a won-derful husband, and you should not monopolize him. "The hard part was that she was much better looking than me," Betsy said. "People used to come up to me and say, 'I feel sorry for you; Sondra's so beautiful.' "

Sally

This story begins nearly 12 years ago, when a troubled young Mormon girl wedded a "wild" young Mormon boy and they began to build their family in the gospel. This couple later converted to the Allred group and brought their family of five children to the northern branch of the group, where they lived in a two-bedroom trailer for 3 months with another fam-ily of three wives and their children. There were 17 people in a two-bedroom trailer. Over the next 5 years, the couple built their own home and had seven different families living at one stage or another in their home with them.

Sally, now 37 years old with eight children, remembers how hard it was to manage with her husband so often working out of state as a drywall construction worker. When they moved into their present home, 6 years ago, which at the time was just a shell of two-by-fours and plywood floors, with no running water or plumbing, Sally had to put up the sheetrock, doors, and fixtures herself. She said she learned about electrical wiring from other women who were doing the same thing and installed her home's lights and plugs. Little by little, she was able to get the home heated with a barrel stove in the basement, floor installed, walls up and standing, and plumbing operating. Some few years later, Sally refused to hand over her earnings to her husband, who was not giving the needed funds for expenses back to her. She was not making enough money to feed and clothe her large family, and she decided to "sin" and keep her own meager earnings for herself and her kids. As a result, she was financially "disowned" by her husband.

During this time, she continued to work on her unfinished home. She and the children often went to the school to shower and used a friend's washer and dryer for dirty clothes. Because the husband was absent for so many years, she had to do much of the parenting herself, as well as the home maintenance. It was during this period that she learned about networking with other women to get by. She relied on one female neighbor to care for her children while she sold Avon beauty supplies in the nearby town. She relied on another woman for "co-oping" with their winter storage supply. She did not raise a garden and the other woman did, and so she would donate her jars and lids in exchange for part of the food grown. She also shared her wood supply with another woman in exchange for some ground wheat.

When Sally moved into her new unfinished home, she remembers relaxing and saying, "I don't have to live with anyone but our family now," but then another family moved in with her. It was a family from Salt Lake City whose mother was working in Utah while her husband and their four children moved in downstairs from Sally. For 4 months, Sally was caring for this woman's children without having met her. This situation was very difficult for her as she had eight children of her own. Another family that moved in was helping itself to the food supply stored downstairs. Sally and her husband had to build this family's home for them to get them out. Then, finally, Sally had her basement for her own growing family.

Shortly after the visiting family left, her husband married two new wives and Sally had to find room for new sisterwives. When another man left his 12 wives, her husband was asked to marry the eldest of the 12 with her six kids, who lived in a fair-sized home across town. Sally's husband then fell in love with the 17-year-old daughter of a prominent councilman and brought her to Sally's home to live. She stayed in a bedroom downstairs for 7 months and then went to live in a large, furnished trailer. A few years later, Sally's husband built her new sisterwife a large split-level home.

Sally remarked that at least now she is not sharing her house with her sisterwife any longer. Sally said the youngest wife was the same age as her own daughter. Whenever the whole family got together, the youngest wife never wanted the kitchen mess; she remarked that Sally should clean up because she had the most children. "My kids resented it, and I did, too," said Sally. Her husband rarely came around even to visit his children when he came into town. Rather, he would stay with his youngest wife. "It's true that a man has a favorite wife. It just so happens that it is not me," Sally said.[19]

Sally complained that she is "bursting at the seams" in her home with her eight children, ranging in age from 1 to 17, and all the housework to do. To pay for the children's schooling ($700 per year) at the Harker Academy, she now cleans house several days a week and sells Amway from her home. She also has learned how to build and maintain a home without the help of her husband and, basically, has been the sole financial support of her family for most of her life. To make ends meet, Sally said she relies heavily on her own industry (maid service and sales), the income brought in by her older daughter, and her female friends in the community for support and companionship.

JoAnn

JoAnn is 50 years old, 5 feet, 6 inches tall with curly red hair, and the first wife of a very outspoken yet loyal convert to fundamentalism. She and her husband were both raised in Utah, fell in love shortly after high school, married in the Mormon temple, and lived in a southern Utah community that was adjacent to another fundamentalist schism group. After 20 years and eight children, they became interested in joining fundamentalism.

"There is a certain plateau that you reach in the Mormon Church, and you can't go any further or they call you a heretic," JoAnn told me. "We wanted more from the gospel . . . we want to live the fullness of the gospel. So we joined the Work."

For JoAnn, this transition from orthodox Mormonism to fundamentalism was extremely difficult, but she said she had the pioneer type of personality that would pull her through anything. She lost her friends, her family disowned her, and she moved to a community (Harker) where she did not know anyone and felt like an outsider. Her husband, too, seemed different, now that he was involved in so many community affairs and was so busy accumulating wives. She could see he was vibrantly happy and enjoyed this new experience, but she felt alone and miserable. With the "acquisition" of the first sisterwife, who was more than 20 years younger, she said she became jealous of the attention the sisterwife was getting from a man she herself had lived with for more than 20 years. It seemed so paradoxical. Yet, she knew she had to keep at it. "No one said polygamy was easy. It is the hardest law to live, but it gives the highest rewards," she said.

After the first year, she learned that sexual jealousies were petty and that she could control her disdain for her husband's divided affections. The real pain came from the differential treatment her husband gave to her children and the new wives' children (a third wife was by then added). This problem was the real bone to pick with polygyny—the inequality of a father's attentions. She noted that her husband could no longer give time and attention to Johnny's needs and that he completely forgot Jennifer's birthday. She felt trapped in a system in which she could not communicate her frustrations to anyone for fear of ecclesiastical rebuke and for fear of jeopardizing her eternal position. She needed friends soon, or she would return to her hometown to be with her relatives, if they would have her.

After several years, a fourth wife, who had cancer and was childless, entered JoAnn's family. She helped to initiate a dialogue with all the other women, which created the needed friendship and vocal outlet for which JoAnn had yearned so deeply. The four women became intimate friends and shared all the tasks and duties of what were by then two households (20 feet apart). One wife agreed to work in a nearby town as an accountant, the other at a supermarket, and a third provided her talents as nurse and medicine cabinet. JoAnn's duties involved the care and teaching of all the children (she also worked part-time in the community's private academy). The women rotated cleaning duties, cooking of meals, and general maintenance projects on a weekly basis. On weekends, they all went out on bulk shopping sprees or to nearby orchards to pick apples or pears for canning. When they could, they would stow away dry and canned food goods for their 2 years' storage. This continual cooperative activity led to deeper friendships between the women. None of them seemed to monopolize the husband, who, as an auto parts salesman (a common occupation in the community), often worked long hours away from home. Thus, the majority of their time was spent working, gossiping, and caring for each other. When tragedy of one sort or another hit the family, it was often the women who had to deal with it, in the absence of their husband. For example, there was a huge forest fire that swept across the Bitterroot Mountains several years ago. The fire came precariously close to JoAnn's home. There was no way to get out all their possessions in time to save them. She said she and her sisterwives got together and prayed for the wind to change. Soon afterward, she said, the fire swept past them, leaving them unharmed. "It was our combined faith that did it," she said.

The first time I met JoAnn was during the Sunday meeting when she stood up and "bore her testimony" of the love she had for her sisterwives. Not one mention was made of her love for her husband or other men of the community. They were not the ones who had "survived" with her from day to day.

Today, JoAnn said, there are still difficult times, but she truly believes in the Principle and that there is no other way that God could teach her to be so completely selfless and giving as by sharing her husband, home, and time with these other women. "I could not have survived this long without my sisterwives to help me through the bad times," she said.

Vi

Vi was a convert to the Mormon church at 17. She later met and married Mormon man who said he had a vision that they were to be sealed together. She found he was too sexually aggressive for her tastes, and their marriage was a poor one. Yet, she said, she persevered and bore him five children, knowing that if she severed this eternal relationship, her own salvation would be in peril. But she felt she did not really love him.

She was a massage therapist by trade and was asked by a polygynist family in the nearby community to help their daughters, who were mentally ill. She and her family became close friends with these people and visited them often. An old friend heard about this association and invited her over one night. They met with two other women, the friend's co-wives, to discuss the gospel. They felt they could trust her to come home with them and further talked about the gospel until late at night. She slept fitfully and saw dark visions of despair all night.

In the morning, the friend's husband, a leader in the Allred group, and another councilman came to give her further word about the gospel and said that if her husband did not join her in the Principle, he would be "replaced." Later, she and her husband attended the group dance and met the prophet, who was very charismatic and convinced her husband to join the group. Yet, she was still not convinced. She knew she had to stick with her husband or lose her exaltation.

> My happiness was not important. I could welcome a sisterwife with open arms. That way, I would not have to have my husband around all the time— he would be satisfied with other women and I could have my celibate life. Women in polygyny when past childbearing are retired like racehorses; I looked forward to being put out to pasture.

She said she joined the Allreds because the LDS church was unchallenging and she longed for the fullness. She said it was a way out of her problems.

When converting to the Allred group, Vi knew she could have been given to another man if her husband did not join. But she wondered about her children. Where would they fit in the eternities? She decided to join the Work and remain married to her husband. A few months later, the priesthood told them that the Lord desired them to sell their home and homestead a desert site that was owned by the priesthood.

> We bought a semi-truck to haul our stuff and lived in an old trailer for several months. There was no plumbing, no electricity, and we had to haul water from several miles away. We had just begun the foundation of our new house when the priesthood asked us to move to Harker. This is how we began our lives in the Work.

Jill

Jill was a 31-year-old Brigham Young University student when she met Erica. They had been taking a religious class together and struck up a close friendship through their discussions of the gospel. Jill remembers her courtship with Erica fondly:

> Erica is just as much a part of me as my husband is. I am married to her, too. We are "one flesh," and I wouldn't dream of hurting my own body. I met Erica before I met my husband. She introduced me to him on campus and suggested we marry. I had been dating for years and was getting older . . . into my 30s. I was tired of looking. When I met him, upon the request of my future sisterwife, I knew he was the one for me. The three of us had meetings together, lessons on the doctrine, and fell in love. Whereas Mark [her husband] didn't show me any romance—kissing, etc.—Erica did a lot of hugging and kissing. She romanced me more than Mark did.

Jill remembers how difficult her life was before Erica and Mark came along. She said that many Mormon women are in the same situation: too old to marry and too spiritual to consider anything but celibacy. Jill said that she was a sexually vibrant and intelligent woman who deserved to be loved and appreciated. She was talented, and all that talent went unnoticed, unobserved, and unutilized. In the Work, she is able to use her talents and share her lives with not only one person—Mark—but also her co-wives. She is eager for Mark to now take another wife for her to befriend. She wants to be able to enjoy the law of Sarah courtship and go out with Mark on dates with her sisterwife-to-be, just as Erika did with her. "I can't imagine any other marriage system for me," she said. "It is the best of all worlds."

Patty

Friendships do not always emerge among wives immediately. Patty, now in her early 50s, recalled that when she first married Larry, Sandra's husband, Sandra did not want this union to be made. For the first 6 months, Sandra refused to speak to Patty. Because Patty admitted she did not marry Larry for romantic love or emotional support but for his testimony of the Principle and economic support of her five children, she especially sought a friend in her first sisterwife, someone to talk to. Sandra finally came around and is now good friends with Patty. They work together closely at the school. After a year of marriage, the two women cooperated on canning and food preparation projects. Yet, they still had some differences to iron out. Then, some years later when Larry died, the two were always seen together and became the best of friends. Patty was left a widow with five kids, the oldest 12, the youngest 18 months. Brother Howard was chosen to propose to her, and she accepted.

This story of Patty and her co-wife, Sandra, was a common one. Many women do not reach a full friendship until they are forced to through economic hardship or until the source of their competitiveness, their husband, passes away. While he was alive, their husband inevitably showed affection to one and not the other. Even the fairest husband has to give his love and gifts one at a time, and the other wife feels slighted and left out. Two strong-willed, outspoken women like Patty and Sandra had a problem. With the problem removed—that is, the death of the husband—the two became excellent friends.

Beth

When Beth married the son of a prominent councilman, she was very happy. She loved Tony, and he loved her. They had two children, and he died suddenly in a car accident, which left her in the care of the councilman-patriarch. The patriarch assigned her to marry his oldest son, the brother of the dead man, for earth "time only" and not for eternity.[20] Contention between this husband and Beth escalated over the years, during which time she bore five more children. Beth decided she could not take it any more and requested a release (divorce) from the eldest son. She and the man both admitted that they did not marry for love but as a council assignment. She became frustrated with her husband's "complacency" about his own children, his inattention to her needs, and his family's differential treatment of her as a time wife. She longed for the past, when, as an "eternal wife" with a man she dearly loved, she had known happiness and acceptance.

All the children born to Beth from the eldest son (her second husband) by right belong to the deceased husband (her first husband), to whom she was eternally sealed. Yet, there is some question as to her rights over her children. She hesitates to leave the area for fear that her children will be claimed by the eldest son and his father, the patriarch, and she will never see them again. Her problem relates to her low status in the family. For example, she was not allowed use the name of her husband, the eldest son, as the name for the son she bore him because she was a "time" wife; the eldest's third wife then later had a son and was able to name him after the husband. She said that she is economically cared for but is manipulated into obedience by the family rule and the concept that women be "seen, not heard" and that all "family" women follow the example of the patriarch's first wife. She wants a release from the family. She said it is too difficult to live with a family with a "God complex."

Some time later, she and her present (second) husband were separated, and he now has stopped visiting his children. The patriarch's first wife tells her that she now will not get to be with her deceased first husband because she asked for a release from her second husband. Her salvation is being threatened, she said. One councilman, the uncle of her present husband, sent her a note telling her not to swear so much. Beth said that the councilman in charge of her release was hesitant to break up her family. He told her that women who get releases are on unstable ground.

> Even if the husband was abusive, she is on shaky ground, because now she has nothing to hold on to. I have granted releases when people were justified, not sanctified. The percentage of women who stay in the Work is small after a release, even if the husband is wrong. Finding happiness again for women after their release is rare. They are not whole again, but half. They have nothing, no man, to lean on.

Beth is resigned to remaining in the community for her children's sake but is not associating with her husband's family. Instead, she has become intimate friends with other women, such as Mary, who understand her situation and offer moral support and friendship to her.

Tina

Tina[21] had been married to a homosexual man in the orthodox church and, in leaving him, found fundamentalism.[22] She and her children attended the Allred meetings and felt they were treated like a long-lost family. The "sisters" of the group began asking her and her children to spend weekends in their homes. The brethren stood off to the side and observed their wives woo her affections toward their families. One woman's husband began wooing her, and then her husband would show fatherly concern for the welfare of her children. Tina's son began being included in activities with the man's sons, and this same man's daughters began taking exceptional care of her little girl.

Tina received keen attention from seven women of stature, the wives of the councilman who was courting her. They were kind to her and shared their knowledge of the scriptures and the gospel, as well as the merits of their husband, who was an apostle of God. They had received a personal revelation with the accompanying "burning in the bosom" of their testimony that Tina and her children belonged in his family. Their testimony was also confirmed as true to them by the prophet himself.

One wife took Tina's children for 3 days and nights while she went alone to a secluded cabin, where she was supposed to received God's word that she should marry the councilman. "I made every effort to be absolutely honest in my endeavor. I prayed exactly as instructed and fasted, I anticipated a vision of some magnitude, and, yes, I finally got the testimony I was seeking."

Early on the fourth morning, seven beaming women and one proud man arrived at the cabin. As soon as Tina opened the door, they began to sing praises to the Lord for her, the new addition to their family. They were so anxious, honoring, and flattering, saying how pure and clean Tina appeared after her marvelous experience. They prepared her to be a new "queen in their husband's hive." No time was wasted in their preparations for her marriage to their husband. Everything was planned and done for her. She and her children were rebaptized, and Tina became the newest wife of an apostle of God.

Tina soon discovered that her husband treated each wife differently, with his first wife ranked as queen above the others. He also became extremely demanding of her and scolded her often for her disrespect of him whenever she made the slightest request or complaint. She found herself praying fervently to God every night, "Help me be good so my husband will like me and help me." This became her sole obsession. When she found that he did not care for her, she turned to another.

Tina found that her best friend in the world and the only person who understood her needs was her sisterwife Joyce. During the delivery of Tina's children, Joyce was there to hold her hand and comfort her; during Joyce's childbirths, Tina comforted her. The two wives were several years younger than the other wives and found that they were much happier living and working together than with the larger family. Their husband did not spend much time with them because they were removed from the other wives, who were higher ranked, and so they spent most of their time just with each other, letting their children play and sleep together as if they were full brothers and sisters.

After the death of one of Tina's babies, she was told by her husband that she was a sinner and that if she had been more obedient to him, the child would not have perished. Because Joyce, her sisterwife, had suggested that the family take Tina to the hospital during her delivery, she and Tina both were banished from their husband's affections. Their children were also taken from them and distributed among the other wives. Tina and Joyce were told to work and provide for the other families and prove their devotion to their husband by showing respect. They did this for a year and then were able to get their children back. During this year, Tina and Joyce hid their misery in each other's love and devotion. "Joyce and I grew to love each other. We shared a mutual hate for our husband and for his lack of attention and help. We often held each other in our suffering to comfort each other. We would lie naked and a fire ignited and we loved each other. We continued to love, comfort and nourish each other."

Tina said for a long time their husband did not visit, nor did they expect him; that no longer mattered. They considered the intimate relationship they shared to be the action of "two desperate souls," hungering for a sense of love and acceptance. This was their special sisterhood.[23]

Dolly

Dolly is now 67 years old and holds one of the most prominent positions in the community: She is the prophet's righthand "man," so to speak. She advises him on every action he takes and directs the affairs of the council, albeit subtly, as the secretary to the prophet.

Dolly was married to a "shady" character in the Mormon church many years ago. She met him at a church dance and he was very charming. Together, they were married in the Salt Lake City temple and through the years, Dolly bore him five children. At age 35, Dolly realized that her husband was going "nowhere" in the church. He was unemployed, he was not active in his callings in the church, and he was drinking beer with his buddies every night. She was dissatisfied with her life with him, and she felt that the church was not recognizing her ability to direct the priesthood in her home as the head of her family.

She converted to the Allred group at 36 years of age, leaving her husband one night after he had been drinking. She did not divorce him legally and to this day is still his lawful wife. She had developed close personal friendships with the Allred prophet's wives, and they welcomed her gladly into their home in South Salt Lake. She chose to marry the second in command, a humble, aging patriarch who had a nice home on the hill by the worship building. She was able to receive her second anointings and become a true queen in Zion. Her children were richly cared for and now are married to respected members of councilmen's families.

Dolly's new husband was growing feebleminded, and she asked the prophet if she could be spiritually sealed to the deceased prophet-founder, Rulon Allred. She was able to get this sealing and was chosen by the current prophet to stand by his side as his assistant. To this day, Dolly continues to direct the activities and organizations of the Allred group. She is a vibrant, strong woman often chosen to speak to outsiders, such as FBI agents, sheriffs, and journalists, when they demand answers from the group.

MANY OF THESE STORIES have been volatile in conveying the wide range of conditions. Admittedly, the gossip channels bore these "fruit" because they were exciting and interesting, not necessarily representative of the whole picture of plural marriage in Harker and the larger group. I found, for example, in my personal inquiries and observations that, of the 25 extended polygynous families that are my main study group, 16 of those marriages were quite successful at creating a desirable environment for both men and women and for all intents and purposes. These families represented the more common patterns of the group. However, I have not lost sight of the other third who expressed dissatisfaction in their marriages and who desired to change their lives by either leaving the system or getting out of undesirable unions.

In short, the patterns I see emerging throughout these narratives are all concerned with women using their relationships with other women to cope with polygynous life. JoAnn leaned on her co-wives for economic and emotional support; Tina used her intimate bonds with her co-wife for a sense of love and warmth when there was no other source of this love. For Betsy and Jill, it was their courtship with their sisterwives that enabled such an easy transition into a polygynous lifestyle.

The stories of women's experiences in courtship and marriage tell us many important things about male-female relationships. We know that some marriages work out and others are doomed for failure. Why is this? I conducted a small survey among 10 women of various backgrounds and personalities to shed light on these questions. I inquired of them all: "What does it take to make a good marriage?" Among the many suggestions given, such as age, abilities, devotion to the gospel, good looks, and personality, the most common answer was "treatment of wife by husband." While some women said that it is the husband who can make or break the marriage, all of the women agreed that the selection of co-wives was crucial to a contented marriage. A further suggestion by many woman was that a particular personality type was needed to endure the difficulties of the polygynous lifestyle: perseverance, fortitude, compassion, frugality, hard work, cooperation, and above all, spirituality. "Those woman who don't have these qualities and come into the Work for sex, money, and full-time male attentions should never have joined in the first place," said one woman.

The results of interviewing wives further indicated that there are stages a polygynist wife passes through in her attempt to find appreciation and self-worth. As one woman described it, "First, a woman will be *tight* with her husband, praying for his love and obeying his every word, at the expense of her own children. Then she will be tight with her sisterwives, praying that they will love and accept her, at the expense of her husband and children. Then, finally, she turns toward her children, realizing they are the ones that really matter."

One Harker woman described her relations with her co-wives as based on the whims of her husband and on inequality of provisions. Another woman, the first of five wives, said that she watched each subsequent wife go through a stage of jealousy and hurt feelings when entering the family. She said that each one thought, when courting her husband, that she would be his favorite and that they left the Mormon church to be "a big fish in a little pond." But soon after the first couple of months of marriage, she said, the wives became relegated to the back burners of family life, no longer able to retain the attention of their husband. They, in effect, became little fish in a little pond.

Another constant point of contention between wives is control over the household, especially if residence is communal. Wives who must live with a first wife in her home—a home that she has worked to improve and manage for many years—often finds her physical space and domestic jurisdiction to be limited. Furthermore, convert women who marry into an established family setting, where the husband and wife(s) are natives of the group, often say they experience alienation and great discomfort. For example, one convert woman said she complained of "spiritual abuse" by her father-in-law, a prominent council member, and his first wife, who was the "queen of the hive." She said they also threatened her with danmation and said that she could leave the group but that her children would have to remain with the family.

Another woman said she felt all alone in the world because she was unable to have children. She loved her co-wives and their support of her but feared the reprimand of the larger established family to which she belonged. It was clear that she could not contribute to the posterity of the clan, and the prominent members of the family reminded her often of her resulting lower status.

Some wives, however, adapted exceedingly well to polygynous life by modeling their relationships with each other as a mother-daughter dyad in which the older wife instructed and patronized the younger wife, still young, inexperienced, and in need of counseling. When the older wife is then older and ill, the younger will care for her. Some wives, closer in age and personality, become instant friends, often having promoted the marriage of their best childhood friends to their husband. These close wives often form unions in opposition to their husband or at least tease him and play practical jokes on him. One woman said, "We love each other more than sisters. We know we will be together throughout eternity. No quarrel is worth ruining that."

In short, many factors are influencing women's decisions to stick with a plural marriage, even when it is clearly a poor one. First, they know that they will inherit eternal worlds where they and their children will be able to live in peace. Some women even suggest that if they can just endure their earthly marriage, they will be rewarded with a man who is much more righteous and understanding in the next life. Second, women know that if they do not work with their co-wives and other women of the community, they will be at a great economic and sociological disadvantage in the community. Third, women realize that there are advantages and "compensations" in the gospel in their relationships with other women, which can make life pleasant and bearable, such as the case of Tina and JoAnn. Those who buck the system, like Beth and April, may be given another chance to marry, but even if their release is granted, which may take years to approve, the woman is placed in a marginalized position in society. If she remarries within a relatively short period of time, she regains her status as a full member of the sect. But if she stays unmarried, her ties with those who wield power in the sect are severed.

Measuring the full extent of Harker marriages would require getting at these negative conditions as well as the actual dissolutions. How common are divorces among Harker residents? Is the rate any higher among monogamous Mormons or monogamous Americans in general? Harold Christensen notes that mainstream Mormons have a divorce rate that is above the national average (1972:21). In other words, how many of these marital problems appear in monogamous culture, and which are unique to polygyny? I suggest that many of the personality differences and poor treatment of women are reflective of the larger monogamous culture as well and are not characteristic of polygny per se. The unique aspect of polygyny, however, is that it provides women with some recourse and respite from their husband, if needed, and allows a built-in system of support and conspiracy that makes life more tolerable for women stuck in a marriage that does not suit them. Also, most of the children have a father figure, even if he is absent.

Differential Access to Values Resources in Marriage Unions

So far, this chapter has shown the wide range of marriage experiences. This last section describes the advantages female converts and elite males have in the system and why women are able to enter the group and settle so rapidly and easily.

Reproductive Advantage

Allredites use elite polygyny as a strategy for control and maintenance of the status quo. It has become a critical mechanism in the development of political exploitation and stratification. Much like in Uganda (Musisi 1991), patron-client (established-convert) relationships within the Allred group create categories of "special women" available for elite marriages. The presence of elite polygyny acts to manipulate the male population so that a small number of elite men have an extraordinary number of wives and the much larger class of low-status men rarely have more than one or two wives. Elite polygyny, in sum, operates in the Allred group to allow small numbers of prestigious male leaders to control the distribution of wives and resources within the community. It also allows a select group of convert women, as the wives of the elite leaders, to control and manipulate the numbers of children born to prominent established families.

There are two measures of this reproductive advantage: (1) number of wives per elite male and (2) number of children born to each wife, related intrinsically to "age of bride at marriage." Table 5 shows the distribution of wives among pure blood or elite men and lower-class convert men. Equal percentages of established and convert males have two wives (45.6% or 128 of 280; 45.4% or 89 of 197), but a significantly larger number of established men (22.3% or 62 of 280) than convert men (8.6% or 17 of 197) are married to three or more wives.

Table 5. Distribution of Wives among Established and Convert Males in the 1993 Census

Male Population	One Wife	Two Wives	Three or More Wives	Total	Average Number of Wives
Established men	90 (32.0%)	128 (45.6%)	62 (22.3%)	280	3.2
Convert men	91 (46.0%)	89 (45.4%)	17 (8.6%)	197	2.4
Total	181 (37.8%)	217 (45.6%)	79 (16.6%)	477	

Table 5 also shows the mean numbers of wives for established and convert males in the 1993 sample. It illustrates the significant discrepancy between number of wives attached to established males (3.2) and number of wives attached to convert males (2.4).

Another point of interest is the equal number of monogamist established (90) and convert (91) men, which suggests that, like convert males, many lower-class established men have not been able to reach the highest levels of kingdom building. There are only a few spots of prestige available, and established men who are not themselves leaders or appointees may be no better off than incoming male converts who vie for power. They are connected through blood, which is valuable and significant, but these lower ranked established men do not access the same valued resources as their more prestigious fathers and older brothers. Rather, they become the supporters and the followers of the system. In short, the system creates an atmosphere of high competition among both established and convert men for the same number of women.

The age of the bride is another measure of reproductive power. Table 6 shows the modal range of age of wives at marriage in a sample of 1,331 wives in 1993. It shows that the largest category of wives, both established

Table 6. Age of Wives at Marriage in Study Population in 1993

Age	Monogamous or First Wife	Second Wife	Third Wife	Fourth or Later Wife	Total
14–19	185 (33.5%)	168 (30.5%)	118 (19.0%)	89 (17.0%)	560
20–29	92 (40.0%)	85 (31.0%)	59 (22.0%)	33 (14.0%)	269
30–39	196 (45.2%)	135 (30.8%)	57 (13.5%)	43 (10.5%)	431
40–50	37 (52.5%)	20 (27.5%)	9 (13%)	5 (7%)	71
Total	510	408	243	170	1331

and convert, married between the ages of 14 and 19 (510 of 1,331). Also of interest is the large number of women who marry after age 30 (431 of 1,331), which suggests that older single women, widows, divorced women, and women who leave their husbands in the mainstream church can find a husband in the group rather easily. Another point of interest is that a significant portion of the third and fourth wives (36%) are marrying as teenagers, and 36% are marrying in their '20s. By contrast, only 30% of the second wives are in the youngest age category (14–19). Teenage first wives are also well under 40%, which to suggests that first marriages are quite close in age and that teenage brides seem to be willing to marry men much older than themselves.

This table also shows that monogamous wives and second wives married at approximately the same age. The ages of these wives at marriage clusters around the 14-to-19 age range. They also cluster around the age category 30 to 39. Why is this? I found that convert women, coming in from the orthodox church, raise the percentage of women who are married in their 30s and 40s. Overall, the data show that both convert and established men were marrying women at a variety of ages.

Women's advantage here is that they can choose to be connected to a powerful elite polygynous man's family. Their reproductive strategies are connected to the autonomy and upward mobility that they achieve in the structure. They can manipulate the numbers of children born to certain families by attaching themselves to those families through marriage and adoption. And, as shown earlier, they are experts at marrying above their own status and at forming a network of women around them to better access valued economic and social resources.

So far in this book, we have looked at the experiences of women in their struggle to make ends meet and settle into the Allred group. The overall picture has been one of leaving the orthodox LDS church for a better life in a new community. The first phase of integration was conversion and commitment, when men and women were asked to consecrate their goods and leave their old lives behind. The second phase of integration was to accept the ideological tenets and adapt individual behavior to these models. Both of these phases favor speedy female assimilation and integration. The third phase (Figure 11) shows how women access more of the valued material and spiritual resources required in kingdom building than men do. An individual's progress traced through the system in the model shows that women, again, have more direct routes to the kingdom. Women come in with men at the start, answering yes to the support of the council and to accessing or generating needed resources; they also can bypass these steps and go directly into celestial marriage to a high-ranked

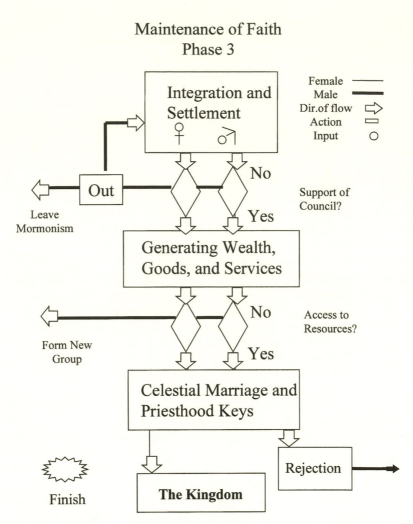

Figure 11. Phase 3 shows how male and female converts have differential access to values resources. Once again, the females—through their close ties to high-ranking councilmen and their access to female economic networks—are able to move more quickly through the system, reaching the final pinnacle, called the "Kingdom." Males relinquish thier valued goods and are less likely to forsake their individuality and align themselves with high-ranking councilmen.

priesthood bearer who has access to valued goods and services. Men, by contrast, more often say no to full deference to the council, find it hard to access valued resources, and more often leave the system rather than reaching the kingdom.

At this stage, male converts are eager to become patriarchs over their own kingdoms, select new plural wives for the production of many children, and exert power and influence over many individuals as the religious and political leaders that they envision themselves to be. Female converts are eager to find righteous husbands and begin raising children in a secure kingdom that contains enough resources to sustain numerous offspring. They adopt the ideals that promote home, family, and marriage to a husband who will take them to the celestial kingdom. They also seek the solidarity and stability they missed in the orthodox church. Male converts, by contrast, must face a contradictory reality that involves severe competition with other men for the same few positions and scant resources. In short, where ideology meets the grounds of social structure and economy, men and women have very different potentials for maintaining stability and commitment.

six

*

Living Arrangements and Individuality

Sharing Space

Women work with each other to accommodate their living needs and are ingenious at creating a home for their children out of the humblest materials. This chapter describes women who built homes and living arrangements in the face of extremely cramped surroundings and scant materials. The patterns here show that women access communal goods and rely heavily on the "sisterhood" for comfortable living.

Creative Homemaking

The following stories show a variety of home-making techniques, most of which require women to scrounge for supplies and force them to deal with another wife's idiosyncracies. In these cases, the true art of sharing is learned. When a need arises, an item or service is provided. When a woman receives another wife into her home, she sacrifices her space, her privacy, and her material goods. Likewise, when a new wife comes into a new family, she must share her wealth and private space with her husband's other wives. Harker women say this is one of the most difficult but rewarding aspects of the Principle.

Yolanda

As a young, convert second wife, Yolonda had virtually no possessions and no money with which to rent a place to live, so she moved into her husband's first wife's rambler (a one-story ranch house with basement) in Harker and was given one-half of the family's basement in which to create

114

her living space. She told me how difficult it was to adjust to the living styles and requirements of her husband's first wife and how hard it was to build a habitation out of nothing. She began living in the L-shaped part of the basement recreation room, where there was a small space for a living room, a potential bedroom, and kitchen (a sink was already present). She and her husband found an old screendoor and mounted it in the kitchen area to seal that part off for her privacy from the rest of the basement. She shared a bathroom, laundry, and living room with the first wife, but she spent most of her time in her own space. She heated with the basement fireplace and put a sofabed in her dining room–bedroom. Two years went by with her eating dinner and sharing bath with the first wife. They shared duties such as "you cook, I'll clean." When the first wife's mother, who did not know of the existence of Yolanda, came to visit, she had to duck downstairs for the whole visit. After that, her husband put a refrigerator downstairs so that Yolanda could be self-sufficient. As the first wife's family grew in size from five to seven, it was decided that Yolanda should move into a small trailer, which had belonged to one of the first wife's eldest daughter who, at 17 had married and moved out of the family home. She later moved to Zion with her husband and baby.[1] The trailer, with a small kitchen, bath, and two bedrooms, is currently sufficient for her needs. Yolanda has two children and is quite comfortable. But when her family grows to three, four, and five children, she said, she will have to find another place to live.

Because of the two women's different cleaning styles there had been friction and constant disagreement in the rambler. Now that Yolanda has her own place where she can have her own style, she said, her relationship with the first wife is much better.

Yolanda says that some women are great at living together. They share tasks and mesh their living styles beautifully. But she has always lived solo, and now that she is in a plural marriage, the best scenario is a solo one. She is sure that God wanted her to live on her own because it best reflects the way that women exist as queens and sovereigns in the afterlife. Women will be expected to be autonomous and independent, guiding and controlling their own "little kingdoms" of children in their own spiritual households.

Margaret

Margaret, now in her mid-40s, desperately wants to live with her other sisterwives who are scattered all the way from Salt Lake City to Harker, over more than 500 miles of territory. She longed for the bonding and spirituality that comes from sharing daily tasks and prayers and songs together. Alone in her small trailer with her three children, she feels like she might as well have been on a distant planet, isolated from the warmth and companionship that other women could bring, not to mention the practical economic and social help they could give to her. She recalls the time when the four wives had all lived together in one split-level. It was crowded, but at least they were together. "Our kids could interact, we had to work out the day-to-day squabbles that make us stronger, better people," she said.

After this early communal experience and the further growth of the family, the wives were separated into two homes with two wives in each. They were then further separated into two states, with one wife in Salt Lake and three scattered all over Harker. "I long for the day when we can live in our communal home," she said. "A family must communicate, eat together, pray together. We must be 'one flesh.' " She described her ideal living arrangement as being a circular home with several separate apartments with kitchenettes and bedrooms all surrounding a huge kitchen–living room area. Each apartment would have separate outside entrances, with an entrance to the communal area in the center as well. The wives would have gardens outside their own apartments. Bedrooms would be modular, accordion-like, on either side of their own living areas. This way the individual families could grow and recede with the number of children living at home. If one wife had three children, she would give some of her bedrooms for a wife with eleven children, for instance. In this way, the sisterwives could get the best of both worlds, she said. They can be individuals and yet be a part of the larger whole.

Melanie

Melanie, like Margaret, wanted to live with her sisterwife to better share tasks with her and be "one flesh." After 7 years of living several miles apart in two trailers, the family succeeded in building a large communal home where both women will have separate dwellings yet live under the same roof. The home is 6,000 square feet on three levels. The basement floor is cement, with a drain to catch water, so that the canning area can be cleaned quickly with a hose. The basement has a recreation room for the children to play in during the long winters. There is also a two-bedroom–kitchenette area for a future third wife to occupy. The first floor has a vestibule for wiping feet, a large living room with a bay window where the family meets for music and prayer, and a large communal kitchen and dining area. There is a pantry for weekly supplies and a bar with stools for fast meals at breakfast. A large, multipurpose coed bathroom with partitions is built across from the dining area, and an 8-square-foot room is just north of that was built only for the father and his things.

The second floor is where the wives' individuality is expressed. It is divided equally into two parts with a connecting hall. Melanie's side is decorated in fall colors in a Victorian style with a connecting sundeck off her master bedroom. She has her own bathroom and an extra bedroom for her three children. Her co-wife's side is decorated in southwestern pastels and has a solarium off her bedroom. She also has a bathroom and two bedrooms for her six children.

> Many of the larger families share separate homes, but that wouldn't do for Stacy and me. When you live together, you have to work out your differences, and that's how you get polished for the kingdom. We are very dear and close friends. And I know that Jack [her husband] loves Stacy, and this fact makes me love him more and her more. We pretty much think alike, there is little or no jealousy. Sure, there are circumstances that come up. But we've had a companionship that other women don't have. I've seen a lot of women be extremely lonely when their husband is out of town. I've been grateful for the companionship we enjoy.

Janet and Hannah

Janet is the third wife of a prominent council member in Harker. Bob has 54 children from six wives, one of whom died. The wives have lived in a variety of configurations and are said to have "grown" from the times when they were communal. Hannah, the fourth wife, said she has been blessed by her association with Bob's other wives but is glad to have her own rather small home apart from them. She said that a large family must be separate to survive and that a good man—and good wives—can achieve unity and spiritual closeness in spite of living in separate dwellings. Hannah said that Bob shows the other wives that he still thinks of them even though he is at another wife's home. He shows affection and calls home regularly. He is also flexible in attending to the wives' needs to be "free of him" during certain periods, such as when they are not feeling like having company, sexual intercourse, or preparing a nice meal. Bob and his family meet all together for family home evening in the large hall in the meeting house once a week, if Bob is in town that particular week.

When Bob and his first wife married, they lived in a little house in Salt Lake City. After a few children, they picked up a second wife who lived with them. The first wife and her children lived in one room, while the

second wife and her children occupied the other. When they moved to
Harker in the 1960s, they had to squeeze into various configurations with
others for a season while Bob built the large, one-story ranch house that
the first wife now occupies. The two wives lived in this home for several
years until the second wife died. She had 5 children, which were then the
first wife's responsibility, who by then already had 10 of her own. Because
of the growing number of children and the additional needs of supplying
space for two more wives, Sara and Janet, the women separated into three
dwellings: the large ranch house for the first wife and her 15 children,
Sara with her birth sister in a duplex built by Bob and his brother, and
Janet in a small one-bedroom cement house that she and Sara had at first
shared with a fourth wife, Hannah.

With the addition of the fifth wife, the co-wives are arranged as follows:
first wife in large ranch house, second wife in a duplex with her birth
sister, third wife in a trailer, fourth wife in a one-room cement block
house, and fifth wife outside the town in a small cabin-style house. Janet's
present constraints are that she has limited space for her five children and
that she works as a nurse, which keeps her away from home. Because of
her physical distance from her co-wives, she has to rely on other women,
her birth sisters included, to help her care for her children and meet her
economic needs.

UNDERSTANDING HOW WOMEN create homes for themselves requires
knowledge of the nature of their dwellings, the size and shape of their
homes, and the jurisdiction wives have over resources.

In a sample of 20 Harker families, I found several dominant patterns
emerging. The first was the single dwelling, which can be called *dyadic*
or *conjugal*, where one wife lives in a dwelling or at least a compartment
separate from other wives, with her own bedroom, kitchen or kitchenette,
bathroom, and parlor of her own. There were many variations of this
theme that overlapped into the second type of dwelling, a mixed pattern,
which combined two single dwellings into one building, such as a duplex
or a main house with an attic apartment. Again, there was much variation
on this second theme. Different types of arrangements are signficant in
affecting female cooperative activity. The most challenging and prestigious was the third configuration, the communal pattern, where wives had
separate bedrooms but shared basically all other spheres of living. In these
situations, women were found to be forced into both cooperative and competitive activities by virtue of their constant "elbow rubbing." In the single or separate dwelling (dyadic), however, there were fewer opportunities

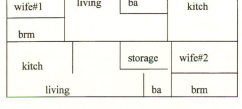

wife#2 brm	kid's brm	wife#1 brm		
ba	kit/ liv	brm	ba	
wife#3 brm	brm	wife#4 brm		
	ba			

Communal

wife#1 brm	kid's brm	
	ba	living

Dyadic/Separate

kitch living	brm	brm	wife#2 brm
		ba	

wife#1	living	ba	kitch
brm			
kitch		storage	wife#2
living		ba	brm

Mixed

Figure 12. This diagram shows three sets of living arrangement styles: communal, mixed, and dyadic or separate. The communal style, which is the ideal, house all wives under one roof, each wife having her own bedroom. The mixed style, which is more common, houses each wife in a separate compartment within the same structure. The dyadic style, which is by far the most common, houses each wife in her own separate dwelling.

for either cooperation or conflict and competition. Figure 12 shows all three living arrangement patterns.

Overall, in spite of the predominant dyadic configuration, I found a rift among the Harker residents as to the proper form of family arrangement (Cannon 1990). One the one hand, there are those like Janet's and Judith's families, who believe in the arrangement of wives in their own separate *dyadic* dwelling or household as soon as they are financially able to do so. On the other hand, there are those such as the families of Melanie and Margaret who believe in the *communal* dwelling, where all wives eventually live harmoniously under one roof. One such arrangement includes seven wives living in one house, sharing one large kitchen and living room area, with separate bedrooms; the children sleep with or near their mothers.

Another family is building a large, prefab, split-level home to house two wives and their children, a place that, ideally, will enable the two wives to more readily share their work such as cooking and cleaning together. For these later families and others like them, the ideal is communal harmony among wives. For the former, the ideal is shared resourcefulness but separate and independent dwellings, which, incidentally, is by far the most common form of living arrangement in Harker (Cannon 1990).

Regardless of the "ideal" of each family's arrangement, the reality of the situation may be entirely different. Because of this incongruity, brought on by financial recession, unemployment, lack of funds, or family size and personality differences, I observed two types of living arrangements within the two "ideal" forms, what I call "house of necessity" and "house of choice." The house of necessity is the living arrangement where wives are in a transitional state of sharing more resources than normally would be necessary because of a lack of funds. JoAnn's family is an example of this type of arrangement. JoAnn's co-wives were forced to live two and three to a trailer in a temporary state of "house of necessity." Their husband was eventually able to build two nice homes to house these wives, and when he acquired a fourth wife, the wives lived two to a home. Yet, these wives are still not in their "house of choice," which will be when all four have their own individual households. By contrast, there is Melanie's family, who were once living separately (JoAnn's family's ideal) but considered themselves to be living in a state of "house of necessity," waiting for their communal home to be finished, which is their "house of choice."

Thus, there are two directions to the movement and history of living arrangements in Harker. On the one side, the *dyadic* families are moving from forced communal arrangements to a more comfortable, agreeable separation of wives. On the other side, the *communal* families may be moving from a crowded, forced communal situation to a more agreeable communal arrangement in a large and spacious home, such as Melanie's family has built.

Because there is no prophet-sanctioned single blueprint for proper living arrangements, there is a discrepancy in the styles and modes of living among Harker residents. One woman stated that new homes are rarely built for two-wife families because the community usually agrees to pay for the first or primary dwelling of a newly wedded couple, not for the families they will be acquiring in the future. Yet, what I see in Harker is a constant transitional state of repair and construction, which leads me to believe that most families are in a state of "house of necessity" moving toward a "house of choice." And, as mentioned earlier, the majority of living arrangements are based on the religiosocial philosophy—possibly adopted because of experienced tension among wives—that each wife have a space of her own, a "room of one's own," a place to work, create, and dwell with her own children. Most of the Harker residents are moving toward this ideal. However, a significant body of members believes in total unity, the concept of unity being complete communality. One woman argued that the concept of unity was not communality per se but of unity in heart and mind and spirit, which occurs only when there exists physical, emotional, and spiritual freedom.

One female informant said that successful living arrangements all depend on what the women can handle in their lives at a given time. "If you can't handle proximity, don't live close to your sisterwife." If you need her resources and company, then live with her. It is as simple as that, she said.

Other factors play a role in co-wife strategies in living arrangements. The lack of privacy or the effect of crowding is a powerful force in the decision-making process. Wives voice discontent if they feel they have lost their individuality. Of course, if it is the husband's will that they grin and bear it for a period, they will do it. For some wives, living and sharing together breeds better relationships, more thorough use of resources, and a more communal atmosphere. But, on the whole, a separate dwelling is the ideal for the wife. There is less tension, less opportunity for quarreling, and more opportunity for a woman's "stewardship" to be expressed.

Other patterns affecting cooperative activity between women is the modus operandi a woman uses to achieve order, whether in communal households or in a completely separate household. I have found that those who live separately limit the extent to which they experience either conflict and cooperation. Separate living further fosters the enhancement of the relationships of a mother to her particular children and to other female allies outside her marriage family.

In sum, like other aspects of Harker, living arrangements are an interplay of ideal and real components, where a husband's perception of his kingdom is the ideal and where co-wives' strategies to meet their economic, sociological, and interpersonal needs are the reality. If a particular style of living arrangement, whether dyadic or communal, meets these needs, it is usually the form that will, in the end, be adopted by the family. This affects female solidarity and cooperative activities in a number of ways. First, if the wives all live together, there may be forced cooperation and sharing by necessity, but there also may be the common problem of "living on top of each other," which may breed contempt and bitterness. Second, if the wives live in separate dwellings, rarely seeing or working with each other, the cooperative networking will more likely occur between women who are not married to the same man but who are conveniently close. Third, women who are living in a mixed configuration of both communal and dyadic features may find it easy to cooperate closely in some areas, such as the sharing of utilities and appliances, but remain dyadic in other areas, such as their bedrooms, parlors, and kitchens. Again, the variety of living arrangements is enormous; it affects female solidarity merely as one factor in many that enables women to rely on each other more so than on their husbands.

In defining men's preferences in living, I found that most men liked the ideal of a large, communal home, where each wife lived in her own enclosed section of the home. In this setting, the ideal is for the man to have his own study or "place away from everyone," where he can read, study, write, pray, or just "veg out." In reality, I found that most men actually were drawn to the dyadic style in which each woman had her own place and the man was able to visit each individually, deal with each woman's problems on an independent level, and simulate the monogamous style, even if just for a few nights.

✳

About Sickness, Barrenness, Aging, and Death

Women generally work together to find solidarity and love in the community. This solidarity is achieved in spite of community norms that shun barrenness and sickness and a structure that criticizes those who cannot pull their own weight. This chapter provides narratives of four women who were able to overcome their dysfunctional status through female friendship and creative stewardships.

More broadly, these stories illustrate how women, when going through the natural processes of life, often find that the best source of comfort during these difficult times is their friendships with other women in the community. These stories are highly representative of women's experiences in Harker. At one point or another, all women experience sickness, aging, and death.

Women in Need

Hillary

Hillary is JoAnn's 31-year-old sisterwife, the one who works in the supermarket as part of her tasks in the family. She already had six children when she suddenly got sick. The trouble began with the pregnancy of her seventh child. She felt great discomfort and sharp pains in her lower abdomen. She could not sleep and was often up at night with sick children. She finally had to stop work completely, which wreaked havoc on the finances of the family. Her other wives had to take on new jobs and find even more creative ways to cut expenses. At the beginning of the third trimester, she felt so much back pain and discomfort that her husband took her to get a checkup with the naturopath that the community often consults in emergencies. He detected signs of placenta previa and recommended that she go right to bed and not leave the bed for the rest of her pregnancy; further, he suggested constant nursing and care be given her in the next few weeks.

Immediately, Hillary's co-wives went to work rescheduling their activities around her, so as to care for her children, clean her portion of the house, and see that she was not put under any undue stress. They took over her duties and prepared for her child's birth, as if there were no question that the child would be born on time and be healthy. When the birth pains came, Hillary felt enormous pain in her lower abdomen and screamed for help. Her sisterwife JoAnn came to her side and comforted her, praying that all would be right. The husband and the other wives came soon afterward, and Hillary was given a priesthood blessing that the child and mother would live. A call to the naturopath was made. He recommended that they take her immediately to the emergency room in the local hospital, as her life was in danger, as well as that of the child. "The cord could be wrapped around the baby's neck, and, in any case, the placenta is blocking the passageway. The baby can't get out," the doctor said.

Hillary's co-wives helped comfort her with raspberry tea and called the midwife for help. Upon arriving, she went right to work on Hillary, using effleurage and other massaging techniques to move the placenta away to allow a free passage for the baby's head. She quickly gave the regular blessing and anointing, as is common with severe cases. After several hours' work, the baby came out, the placenta all distorted and squashed. It was a beautiful, healthy baby girl with dark hair and eyes. Not long afterward, Hillary's own health became better, and she was able to get back to her normal activities.

Ann

Ann is now 65 years old. She is of Swedish origin, with a tall, thin frame and fair skin. Her hair is completely white and quite long, always worn in the typical fundamenalist bun with bobby pins and the sausage curl in front. She recalled how she had been a member of the LDS Church for many years, went on a mission to Venezuela, and attended Brigham Young University. She was 35 when she joined the Work, marrying a man 3 years younger than herself who already had two young wives. One of the wives, a 23-year-old, had two beautiful children. "Oh, how I envied her!" she said. "I so wanted to have children of my own to fill my husband's kingdom."

The other, a 19-year-old then, was pregnant with her first child. Over the first few years, it became apparent that Ann was barren. Various tests were conducted and remedies and blessings given, but, after the fifth year of marriage, Ann knew that she would never become a mother. It was at that time that her status and role in the community shifted. She felt like everyone *knew* she was barren, and, therefore, she had become a nonentity. She went from working with the young children in a religious organization for children to holding a position as town recorder. In the family, she felt estranged from her two younger, fertile sisterwives, and there seemed to be a big rift between them in other ways.

Ann said females are taught from childhood that the greatest virtue in life is to give birth to one of the Heavenly Father's spirit children. They are taught that "children are a heritage of the Lord, and the fruit of the womb is his reward" (Psalms 127:3). Women who cannot have children and yet still live within the system are bitterly reminded of the words of Rachel, Jacob's wife, who when she discovered she was barren said, "Oh give me children, or else I die" (Genesis 30:1). She said that if a woman happens to become barren or infertile before bearing her heavenly quota, she may experience a nervous breakdown or depression.[1] She felt her husband did not give her the attention he gave the other wives because they bore him sons and daughters to fill up his kindom and she did not.[2] She was lonely and miserable.

After about 7 years of marriage, however, another wife was added to the family—a wife who seemed to be the answer to Ann's prayers. Ann loved her immediately. She was friendly, hopeful, anxious for life to begin, and, above all, she did not shun Ann because of her barrenness; on the contrary, she allowed Ann to take care of her children and be a part of their lives. Ann said that she began to live vicariously through the other woman's experiences as a mother. The two women became very close, and this relationship fostered others like it. Ann became active in the Relief Society program (the womens' religious organization), she was known in the town as producing the most beautiful knitted afghans, and she was invaluable in the network in her role as one of the main telephone conduits for spreading vital messages throughout the village.

She told me that, had not have been for this co-wife, she would have soon left the Work, which would have jeopardized her eternal position. In effect, that co-wife, Ann told me, was her "Savior on Mt. Zion."

Emily

Emily is now 72 years old. She was one of the former prophet's many wives and lived in a trailer one-half mile north of town. She had arthritis quite early on in her life and, because of it, needed help with many of her daily chores, especially in getting to and from the many religious meetings. Most of her co-wives lived in Salt Lake City, and because of this distance Emily was not able to tap into her network and enjoy the association of other women. She felt alone and angry that she was stuck up in Harker.

Emily is a talented Mormon historian who has written many unpublished manuscripts on fundamentalism and on the Allred group. She is extremely bright and has a wealth of information to share. She is also a very bitter and unfriendly woman. She has a great deal of resentment toward many of the men and women of Harker because she says they do not "fully understand the gospel." Nonetheless, she feels the Allred group is the closest thing on earth to God, and so she is determined to stick with it until death.

Her loneliness affected her life in Harker. She recalls the many years she was ignored and muted. When she had just turned 65, however, only a few years after her husband's death, a prominent member of the Harker community asked if he could be her "time husband," and she agreed. He became her "proxy" priesthood head, giving blessings and economic provisions for her when needed. His wives thus became her new sisterwives, and their children began calling her Aunt Emily. Because of this surrogate family, she always had plenty of people to drive her into town to replenish her supplies, help her light up the fire every morning, or keep her company on a lonely night. She has grown to accept her position as an adopted member of this family. Several new kinship ties are formed each year surrounding this adoption; a son-in-law who marries into the family also calls her Aunt, or a child born to a sisterwife calls her Grandma. She said she still looks forward to governing over the Allred kingdom when she meets her eternal husband in the next life, but she now finds life worth living because of her associations with her "proxy" sisterwives and the bonds she builds with their children as a surrogate grandma.

Judy and Elaine

Before Elaine died of ovarian cancer, she asked her sisterwife Judy to take her seven children into her home and raise them as if they were her very own. Judy agreed to this, in spite of having her hands full with her own four young children and an income that was barely adequate for her own needs. Elaine told Judy she would die happy knowing that her children would be taught the "proper gospel" and her (Judy's) rewards would be doubled because of her sacrifices. At Elaine's death, it seemed the whole family would fall apart with grief. Here was a loving, exceptional mother, who gave everything for her children and was now gone. Judy stepped right in and took over the duties of dual motherhood. She welcomed the grief-stricken children into her home and did what she could to make the transition easy. The fact that they always called her Aunt Judy, and had already grown to love her as their second mother prior to their own mother's death helped ease this transition greatly. Much of their lives had been spent playing with Judy's children after school or listening to her play the piano during family home evening. They already loved her splendid Swedish pancakes and were familiar with the "spirit she emanated." After a period of a few years, the older children left the house, and the younger ones lived for a while with the other sisterwife, the first wife, Sherry, in her home. This wife was not able to take in the children at Elaine's death because she had eight children of her own, most of them still quite young. Elaine's younger children already loved this first wife as a second mother and were familiar with her wit and humor and her deep blue eyes that always seemed to sparkle.

Not long after Elaine's death, one of the husband's brothers got sick and died, leaving a wife and five children behind. The Allred group observes the levirate rule of marriage, which obliged brother Melvin, the husband, to marry his brother's wife, Gertrude, for "time." When he did so, his wives welcomed her into their network as if it were the most natural thing to do. She recalled that they made her feel at home during her grief and made the transition for the children "slick and easy."

In short, these stories of Elaine, Judy, and Gertrude and, for that matter, those of Ann and Hillary, illustrate one of the direct advantages of the polygynous system—positioning after the death of a loved one. These stories show how co-wives can fill in as surrogate mothers and surrogate sisterwives when the regular support system shuts down because of death or abandonment. They are vital in understanding the value of the female network. As with economic and ritual contributions, the means by which women alleviate the normal crises of life for other women and their children keep running the machinery of the network. It turns on and runs when a need arises. One woman told me that she would be helpless without the network. In her family, like JoAnn's, she has the task of caring for all of the children during the workday. In exchange, the other wives maintain the home and bring the supplementary income needed to sustain the household. In addition, one sisterwife cooperates by being the family pediatrician (her children are always sick, so she keeps a stethoscope and ear probe in her home), another is the trauma or blood nurse, another is "wonderful" at soothing children (when one wife's girl got hypothermia and the mother couldn't warm her up, the other could), and still another is the storyteller of the family. In all, she said, "Our children get the best care any one mother could give because we are four mothers doing the job."

eight

*

The Nature of Female Relationships and the Network

Women form associations to create an environment of interdependence, female autonomy, and female satisfaction; this aspect of female satisfaction is vital in the overall picture of female advantage in the system. It explains why women from the mainstream world are attracted to polygyny and how they are able to survive, once baptized, in a dominant male structure. The following pages describe the exact nature of female relationships and networking by providing qualitative analysis and diagrams of network ties among women. The chapter also illustrates the strength of the network ties that women have with each other. Finally, qualifications for successful female networking are described, showing how some women are not suited for the network and how the structure works to "weed" out these women.

The women described in this chapter rely on their associations and networks with other women to cope with their paradoxical existence. They form associations that are made up of many different bases: economic, spiritual, and, in some cases, physical or sexual. Additional factors are family size, living arrangements, the number of co-wives, husband-absence patterns, visiting patterns, allocation of resources, health needs, belief patterns, and emergencies. A woman in need, for example, often networks with other women to buy in bulk, collects supermarket discards, trades labor, and bargains for what she needs to feed and clothe herself and her family. A woman in need of help in managing and maintaining her household networks with other women who are specialists at putting up sheetrock, fixing a clogged sink, or repairing a broken-down stove pipe. A woman in need of medical help goes to the community midwife or other female in-house specialists for herbal remedies and treatments. And a woman in need of physical companionship goes to her sisterwife or another female friend for warmth, love, and a sense of security that is not found with her husband.[1]

In short, women are successful in their network because their husbands do not provide the emotional and economic support needed. They are much like the Iroquois women (Leacock 1978) who were forced into an economic and social interdependence during the long absences of their husbands and brothers, the Mundurucu women of Brazil (Murphy and Murphy 1985), or the Iranian women of Deh Koh (Friedl 1989) who spent most of their time working, playing, raising their children, and living with other women because they were not allowed involvement or advancement in the male sphere.

Associations and Networks

Although kinship looms large in the choices men and women make in Harker society—the very base of kingdom building being fortified with important blood and affinal ties—what becomes increasingly more prominent in the maintenance of the community is the creation of voluntary associations made up of kin and nonkin individuals. It is the utilization of female cooperative associations, in fact, that separates the Harker community not only from other fundamentalist Mormon groups such as Short Creek but also from its own headquarter branch in Salt Lake City.

Harker women's associations or networks are, by nature, flexible social entities in that they are easily founded and easily ended. Just as there are fissions and fusions at the level of the high council (Bennion 1996), there are fissions and fusions in female associations. Women, in this sense, are seen as political actors in a different arena from the male priesthood political world, yet they engage in many of the same manipulations and bargaining tactics to maximize their desired ends.

The purpose of female associations and networking is social solidarity, economic stability, spiritual exchange, and companionship. I relate this definition of *networking* to the concept that was built upon Marcel Mauss's term "the gift," where reciprocal exchange is based on obligation, motive, generosity, and morality (Langness 1987). Each woman in Harker has social relationships with a number of friends and acquaintances, including those individuals with whom they *must* work to achieve their goals. All these relationships together constitute what Wheeldon (1969:132) and Barnes (1954) call a personal network. Relationships between women often differ in their content and complexity. If the situations in which they habitually see each other are clearly distinguished, it is possible to separate, very crudely, the *strands* that contribute to their relationship. For example, if Alice sits with Mary at the Sunday meetings, they are both members of the same wheat-grinding co-op, and, further, they engage in gossip for several hours on the phone several times a week, then I describe their relationship as multiplex or multistranded, having at least three strands: religious, economic, and gossip-friendship. But if Alice sees Mary only at Sunday meetings, then the content of their relationship is likely to be largely determined by this fact alone—joint membership in the same church—and is a uniplex or single-stranded relationship.

Communal sisterhood is not trivial to the female network. Women, in general, have significant bonds with others in the community based on their common personalities, hobbies, and problems. Often, a woman with a certain gripe or grudge or, for that matter, a common characteristic (like being one of the few monogamous women in the community) seeks out other like women. Because women in the community are considered "sisters in the gospel," they are nearly as close as true sisters would be. Women, in general, share in the economic networking of the community and in the healing and praying in the Sunday meeting, the delivery room, and their own testimony meetings. Polygyny becomes an important fact in co-wife relations and community-women relations. Both types of relations are founded in the fact that they share husbands, are living at or below the poverty level, and have the same belief system, which reinforces them as wives, mothers, and members of the community. By polygyny's very nature, these women are forced to rub elbows with each other in everyday life, in motherhood, in homemaking, and in religious worship. They use their own language and know just how to manipulate each other gregariously through communal sharing and service.

I have found the main strands of network content—co-wife, economic, spiritual, physical, blood, and friendship relations—to be representative of *most* women's experience in their associations with other women. Perceiving of women's connections with each other as strands in a network is useful in understanding their relative satisfaction and autonomy in the system. The personal networks among women range from multistranded links with many individuals, indicating high a level of wide-reaching cooperative activity; multistranded links with only one other individual, indicating a high level of narrow-range cooperative activity; and single-stranded links with sisterwives, indicating little cooperative activity. Women with multistranded links to at least one other woman in the community more readily than those with fewer links achieve their economic, spiritual, and sociological goals through the female network With men,

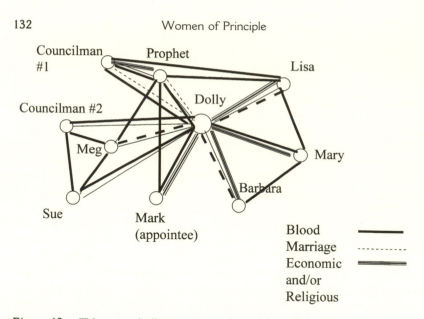

Figure 13. This network diagram shows the multiplex links that one woman, "Dolly," has with the prophet and other key members of the council and their wives. Dolly's strength lies in the nature of her many cross-cutting ties, encompassing vital areas such as economics, blood, marriage, and religion.

for the most part, they share uniplex or single-stranded ties (Gluckman 1967).

Figure 13 shows how—Dolly, the prophet's spokeswoman—shares numerous cross-cutting ties not only with important elite leaders but also with a cluster of women who are also connected to these elite leaders. Together, these women share the common strands of marriage, blood, and economic resources, which create for them a reliable and stable environment for themselves and their large families.

Longevity and Staying Power

Women's networking abilities relate directly to the strength and longevity of their position and status in the community. These abilities also tell us something about their relative satisfaction in society; why would they stay if they did not find something there to keep them? In a sample of 1,024 individuals (597 females, 427 males) who converted to the Allred group from 1953 to 1993, more than 35% (360 individuals) were recorded as having left the group. Of that 35%, more than 72% (250 individuals) were male.

Out of those 664 who stayed in the group, more than 73% were female (487). Only 26% of the converts who stayed on and tried to integrate were male. Even they, however, were not as successful at assimilating as the convert women. For example, taking the sample of 177 male converts who did not leave, only 15 individuals were considered, through an analysis of their economic and social status, to be highly successful in integration. Yet, more than 162 males fit in the category of middle to low integration success, meaning that these individuals failed to integrate successfully and obtain a financially and socially secure position in society. Individuals in this category would be more likely to apostate, become disgruntled, and eventually leave the group.

The women, by contrast, were more successfully integrated. Again, this does not necessarily mean that they were happier with their position, as in the case of women who cannot leave the group because of their fear of losing their children, but it means that these women are more mobile and less likely to apostate than the men are. Of 487 female converts, 240 individuals were considered highly successful in integrating, meaning that they were in a position to benefit financially and socially and/or were not allowed to leave. Only 239 individuals fit in the middle to low integration category, and of them, only 37 fit in the very low category.

In light of these differences between male and female longevity in the group, several tentative conclusions appear warranted. First, happiness and successful integration are two different types of judgments. One plausible interpretation is that satisfaction judgments reflect equity and emotional happiness, whereas integration can be interpreted as assimilation into the mainstream and some degree of insider mobility. This point is vital for understanding the pressures and constraints placed on women to remain in the group whether they are "happy" or not. Once inside, women often remain loyal to their husbands and the group because they are threatened with losing their children and their place in the heavenly kingdom if they defect. Male recruits, however, are encouraged to leave the group but do so recognizing that their possessions, wives, and children will more than likely remain with the group.

Second, it seems that men and women interpret happiness and successful integration quite differently. Women more than men distinguish the two. They, for the most part, equate successful integration with service, sacrifice, and spiritual rewards, rather than notions of supreme power, wealth, and thrones. Albeit, there were many women in the sample who

pursued wealth and power, but, on the whole, most female recruits defined
their integration process by the degree of spirituality and heavenly gifts
they expected to receive. Men did not distinguish personal happiness and
comfort from successful integration but considered the two to be equiva-
lent.

For example, many in the sample suggested that their success was defined by the size of their family kingdom, economic stewardship, and rank
in the system. Obviously, many of these conclusions must be considered
speculative, given the constraints imposed by the interview methods. Individuals may have not told me their true desires and conditions; likewise,
information received in gossip circles about individuals may not have been
completely flawless. Nonetheless, there are clear differences in these data
between the desires, interpretations, and experiences of male and female
recruits.

Thus, the recruitment-integration process in the Allred group favors
lower-class female recruits and upper-class established males and their
convert appointees. Lower-class male recruits do not enjoy relative mobility in the group, nor do lower-class established younger men. Equilib-
rium established in the group is attributed to a number of factors:

1. Flow of female converts into the group
2. Flow of surplus male competitors out of the group
3. Kingdoms are headed by elite priesthood leaders and their eldest
   sons and wives
4. Disengaged male recruits' resources (property, homes, priesthood
   offices, stewardships, wives, and children) are redistributed to
   men and women who have successfully integrated and are on
   their way to building kingdoms of their own, all of which is
   authorized and regulated by the elite priesthood leaders of the
   group.

Female Status

In the course of my research with the Allred group, I have conducted
many studies of relative female status. I compared a sample of Allred
women with a sample of mainstream LDS women and found that Allred
women contributed more to social production, religious ritual, and the
belief in a female deity (Bennion 1996). The problem with searching for
female status in a patriarchal community is that the women themselves do
not necessarily promote it, and, therefore, it is often difficult to evaluate.
There are some interesting patterns, however, that I have observed. They

are features of life that involve work patterns, visiting patterns, hyper-gamy, polygyny, religious ritual, and kinship. As hypergamy, kinship, and polygyny were already discussed in previous chapters, I will focus on working and visiting patterns and solidarity through ritual.

Female Work Patterns

Polygynous women often learn to be flexible by adjusting to different sorts of tasks as part of the dynamics of polygynous life. Mary Catherine Bateson describes this type of flexibility and the conflict that women in general have between work, home, and family.

> Women have always been torn. We forget that when a woman who's been married for a period of time gives birth to a baby, she has to serve two masters. She has to respond to two different kinds of needs. Then she has a second baby. She's got one baby at the breast and one baby on her knee, and they're quite likely to be quarreling. So the traditional feminine roles as wife and mother of multiple children have involved caring for multiple issues, balancing them off, not neglecting that while you're caring about this, having one rhythm to respond to a husband and another one with an infant and another one with a growing child.
>
> This is what it is to be a woman. And this is what it is to keep a household going, *to have multiple skills, to deal with transitions to deal with the health of the whole. There is a sense in which women have retained the capacity to be generalists, to live in an ecology in which there is more than one life and you have to balance them.* (Bateson 1989:165, emphasis added).

The central maxim in working patterns—whether at home or in the marketplace—is that an increased number of wives provides for an in-creased association and communitas for the individual wife; however, proximity of wives can result in increased conflict, increased cooperation, or both. Because polygynous women distribute tasks—tasks that a mo-nogamous woman would be performing alone—there is simply less work done per person.[2] I found this to be the case among only a few households who had succeeded in having a highly coordinated system of cooperation and networking. This is in contrast to the long 10-hour days—and often when meetings are held, 13- or 14-hour days—the male head puts in per day. In short, female networking, for some households, provides Harker women with more time per day to complete a variety of tasks. Ideally, it provides them with more visiting hours and more time to nurture children. It also provides them more time to develop their own talents and hobbies. Most important, the network brings them together in a tight-knit female group, where women associate and mix with other women in mutual aid and worship. Again, this is the ideal, and only a small percentage of women in my sample enjoyed "leisure." As one woman put it, every day is like a "multiheaded monster," with no reprieve from "work, work, work." This same woman agreed, however, that without the help of her female friends and co-wives, the monster would "devour her completely."

One aspect of female work patterns is that in many households there is a modus operandi among co-wives by which the various talents and abilities (and temperaments) of each wife is gleaned and grounded in particular, specialized tasks. Often, the more aggressive wives dominate the shier ones, creating a pecking order. If this pecking order is based on friendly rivalry and a general feeling of equality, there is a better chance that all wives will work well together. If there is an unequal distribution of resources and overt favoritism on the part of the father, then this harmony breaks down. One woman said that her husband often gives in to the most insistent wives, and in the process he shortchanges the reticent ones. In another case, one wife has the monopoly of caring for the husband's clothes and personal belongings, which makes the other women jealous. The others then began to "slip over to grab fresh clothes for their husband before the other wife was awake. It became a game of wit and nerve" (Soloman 1984).

Another aspect of the female working patterns that affects the network is women's work outside the home. Of monogamous and polygynous wives in a contemporary setting, more polygynous wives work outside the home, either in community work or marketplace work (Murphy and Murphy 1985). And those who do not work for wages help support their families by frugally budgeting the goods their husbands provide them. Polygyny in Harker, as elsewhere, develops independent women who bear much of the financial responsibility for their families (Goodson 1976). As a group, they are seen as both good mothers and good providers, good teachers and companions, good cooks and good seamstresses. A common thread runs through all women in Harker that is an integral part of each woman's psychological makeup. A Harker woman is extremely thrifty and hardworking. She has learned this through budgeting her scant resources.

Visiting Patterns

Most social interaction among men occurs in church and civil meetings; after job, chores, and church responsibilities are completed, there is little time for visiting. For women, the social interaction is extended to household, community, and school working tasks, as well as gossiping at the store, talking long hours of the day on the telephone, chatting at church meetings, and taking outings and shopping trips at various times during the week. Women combine visiting with work and, thus, have more social contact with other women than men do. Formally, women visit other women under the auspices of a religious duty in the Relief Society organization called "visiting teaching," in which two women teach another woman preassigned doctrinal lessons once or twice a month. Informally, woman meet with other women many different times a day in a number of settings, to pick up or drop off a child at school or childcare; to plan, budget, or organize some community or family event, such as dinners, parties, home improvement, food preservation, or some other house project; to plan or organize some religious function or activity, such as primary school, Sunday school, Young Women's, Relief Society, or testimonial; to visit-teach; to talk or gossip on the roadside, at the post office, or at the Harker mercantile; or to meet together by nature of living together under the same roof in cooking, cleaning, and childcare tasks.

As a qualifier, I did observe male bonding activities and found them to be less pervasive and enduring. For example, I observed men interacting after a Sunday meeting. They began discussing the proposed water project for the month in the foyer of the meeting house. After a few minutes, there was an argument about task assignment, and the group dispersed. On another occasion, I observed men talking in the cabinet shop about how the government "was screwing all of us." This was a very passionate, adamant discussion. But, just as in the foyer of the church, there developed an argument, and the men went their separate ways. I am confident that there is male bonding surrounding sports and perhaps national politics, but the nature and structure of family life do not permit men the time for much gossiping because they are always at work, on the road, working on priesthood assignments, attending meetings or visiting wives and children.

The paths of women's visiting patterns vary, but on the whole they follow the direction of other sisterwives' houses and quarters, the school-church complex, and the post office–store complex. The amount of visiting among co-wives is much greater than among women in general, but because of the extended need for economic, social, and religious services, there is a great amount of visiting among female community members regardless of whether they are related.

Gossip sessions while visiting are extremely important. For one thing, women often spend most of their time gossiping "someone else's garbage" and, in so doing, make their own situation seem less strained and miserable. Although much of the gossip is of a negative nature, it often succeeds in defining more intimate relationships between the gossipers (Gluckman 1963). Gossip functions to define or reaffirm the norms regulating behavior among members of the same group and marking them off from others, such as the men or the women who are not involved in the network.

Religion and Married Life

Women's religious experiences have been underestimated in much anthropological literature because it is believed that women are prisoners of a male religion (Christ 1980). Women are members of a religion that is theologically dominated by males. This does not mean they are misled in their belief or cajoled by men to believe in a certain way. Women in Harker are devoted members of the religious group because they have a spiritual communion with other women who believe as they do. According to Sinclair (1986), women's position in religious systems is often a reflection of women's status in society, yet religious experience frequently establishes a dimension that is absent in the more restricted secular lives of most women. Because the women are unable to be involved in the higher priesthood ordinances and authority structure of their religion, they must establish a level of religious activity in and among themselves.

Through their belief and commitment to their religion, to their children, and to the concept of their royal destinies, Harker women often express their "unity" and "eternal round" in sisterhood. Seeing other women stand up in church meetings to tell others about their convictions of "truth and righteousness" is a powerful peer tool in uplifting women, each woman becoming part of a continuing round of strengthening and being strengthened. These testimonials are a vital aspect of women's involvement in informal ritual.

Almost every Sunday, during the meeting of the sacrament, several women walk up to the pulpit or stand where they have been sitting in the pews and bear witness to their beliefs. On the second Sunday I was in Harker, for example, two women rose and spoke "with the Spirit." One woman, in her 20s, a mother of three, spoke for 10 minutes about her sisterwives. She pleaded with the Lord to bless them and keep them from harm. In closing, she admonished all women to do the same. The other woman bore her testimony of the Spirit of Christ, which she said had accompanied her in preparation for that moment. She seemed to speak mostly to a row of women, her sisterwives, in front of the pulpit, many of whom were crying uncontrollably. Soon, she, too, was crying and had to sit down without finishing because she was so overwhelmed. This type of belief ritual is common among women, and it is the ritual that many use as a test of faith and commitment to the sisterhood.

In sum, the most important functions of female networking in Harker are to allow women to survive economically and emotionally, provide them with staying power, allow them some modicum of status, and provide for the sustenance and rearing of the large numbers of children. It functions to provide an alternative to the priesthood powers that the men wield and to promote female solidarity.

Whereas many American monogamous women have few bases for building relations with other women, by contrast, the Harker woman is strongly compelled to join in female cooperative activities out of economic need and for spiritual support. Furthermore, whereas a monogamous American woman in her interaction with her husband has little support from others (especially in abuse cases), at the first hint of trouble or sorrow, a Harker woman talks about it with her sisterwives or female friends through the gossip channels and telephone grapevine in the community. One woman told me that if the husband is to blame for some problem, the wives collectively express displeasure at his actions and that, if he is smart, he will change his ways.

Although the average American woman may have a higher official status, the Harker woman is far less directly dominated or individually coerced by a husband. The Harker women are protected by their unity, while other American women are separated from or pitted against one another (Murphy and Murphy 1985:221).

Thus, Harker women find a cohesive core in work, polygyny, the opposing unity of men, kinship, and, in some cases, residence. In short, the network is a vital, equalizing element in Harker society. It supports the patriarchy, builds stable and long-lasting female groups, socializes the town's children, and provides a supplementary source of economic support for the welfare of the entire community.

Qualifications to Female Cooperation and Use of the Network

There are exceptions to any rule. In this case, those women who do not participate well within the network, though fewer in number, are as outspoken as those who want it to work.

Family size, age, economic status, interpersonal differences, and differences in doctrinal interpretations are among the striking factors that promote distance between women. In a study of co-wife living arrangement strategies (Cannon 1992) for example, I noted that the ideal often contradicts reality. The same is true of the female network. On the whole,

it is based on an ideal of harmony and cooperation and is quite commonly
found to be the basis of community support and maintenance. However,
numerous forces can play against this ideal, which cause some women to
separate themselves from their co-wives in order to satisfy their emotional,
psychological, and, sometimes, economic needs.

Pride is of particular importance in understanding the separation between the ideal and the real. When one woman watches another woman
discipline *her* children in a way contrary to what seems reasonable, disputes arise. Sharing tasks and space is one thing, but sharing the elements
of one's own identity, such as the jurisdiction over one's own children,
the arranging of one's room or rooms, and the utility of the products of
one's labor, is often the source of family disruption and turf wars. The
ultimate example of interpersonal tension among co-wives living together
without a space of their own is during personal visits with friends and
family, where a wife's dwelling and bedroom are one and the same. The
bedroom becomes a prison and a multipurpose center all at once. It becomes the only place wives can entertain their guests, pray and discuss
the gospel with their children, and work on sewing and maintenance projects.

When it comes to the survival of one's children, however, pride is no
longer a compelling factor in inhibiting a woman from utilizing the female
network. A proud woman will take the offering of extra food or storage
from a woman she despises in order to feed her hungry children. Likewise,
a woman who has differences of opinion with another woman will more
likely than not lend her money for groceries when asked.

Another negative effect on female cooperative activities and co-wife
relationships is advertising and "the American spirit of capitalism." When
wives view the spacious homes and abundance of goods often found in
nearby towns and cities and in women's home and fashion magazines, I
have observed they become keenly aware of the deficit of their own surroundings. Psychological effects from the outside can be devastating to
young second and third wives, newly married, who must often occupy
temporarily the basements and attics of the first wife's home and manage
with fewer goods and services to match her smaller family.

An additional influence from the larger culture that affects co-wife relations is the introduction of Amway marketeering to Harker. The second
year of my research, this phenomenon was becoming quite widespread.
Several men have recently joined with their first wives in a sales partnership in attempt to provide extra income for their families' needs. It requires
extensive paperwork, household space, and travel to various cities and
states. The result of this enterprise for some families I talked to is that

second and third wives feel estranged from their co-wives who accompany their husbands in this pursuit of additional funds. In many cases, the first wife's income increases, providing her with a larger home apart from the other wives, while the second and third wives' financial status remains unchanged. This relates directly to the ability of co-wives' ability to work closely together in the network. Often, when a grudge is held by one woman against her co-wife, she finds other women in the community who share a similar problem and rally with them against this co-wife.

One of the biggest effects of variability in co-wife relations is the demographic condition of the individual family—that is, the number of children per wife. Regardless of how determined a family is to heed the righteous communal manner of living and be of "one flesh," if there are four to five wives with six to eight children each living under one roof or at least sharing much of the space, the family tends to move in the direction of dyadic, separate living spaces for the wives, with the wives altering their participation in the network to accommodate their individual needs. Furthermore, many first and second wives complained that they "got along famously" until their husband married a third wife. Her presence was like a putting a "wrench in the works."[3]

Another qualification to the women's network is that most women agree that a "good man" can be the turning point in co-wife relations. If a man is a good organizer and is helpful in providing material and spiritual comforts, then co-wives tend to work well together. A husband who is not a good provider and is rarely present but avoids pitting wives against each other through game-playing tactics and the like can be considered a good man because he does not interfere with the wives' ability to work well together. The biggest sin a man can commit, according to many, is to speak about one wife's sexual, emotional, and social idiosyncrasies and faults with another wife, show affection in public to one wife in the presence of another wife, or court other women without the knowledge of his wives.

When a husband shows favoritism among his wives, he breeds discontent among them, and often women fight each other to get the desired attention and valued resources from their husband. For example, often the threat of displacement by another wife may dog the lives of first wives or favorite wives. Because of this, some wives strategize by displaying overt affection, doing special favors, and performing household and wifely duties for the husband to a high degree of satisfaction. However, when the husband gains a new wife or is no longer interested in the first or favorite wife, she often alters her strategies toward more cooperative interaction with her co-wives. Because he is no longer giving her physical and material attention, she may transfer her love from the husband to her children or other women. Thus, if a husband exerts his power and influence on a daily basis or if his power to give or withhold rewards is a vital factor in the prestige and status of his wife and children, the ability of women to work well together can be greatly affected.

Another element of female interrelationships is that most women are juggling two selves in one body. Kimball Young (1954) recorded patterns of both competition and cooperation in his sample of Mormon polygynous women's activities. He suggested that women are affected by the "spirit of capitalism" embedded in American society and feel especially threatened when another wife is found to be a better wife, mother, cook, or bed partner than herself. Because the plural wife depends chiefly upon the pattern of monogamy to guide her in her relations to her husband and her co-wives, she often finds herself split in two. On the one hand, she is supposed to carry on certain duties such as housekeeping and childcare and is the sole sexual partner of her husband. On the other, with polygyny, she is loaded with additional tasks such as subsistence work, household maintenance, and child rearing, plus the sharing of her husband with other women and the sharing of properties among them.

The reconciliation of these divergent ends and means might take place outwardly yet with certain costs of compulsion from outside and certain headaches from within the family. The women are forced into cooperative activities yet often house a contempt for one another. This is the nature of the female split personality in Harker society.

Summary

Based on my observation of female relationships, I have found a number of factors that determine whether women will pursue cooperation or competition: the scarcity of resources (e.g., attention from husband, household goods, and celestial glory, whether this resource is something that could be shared, the personality and background of the individual, (e.g., whether they come from a convert or established family or like to dominate or be submissive), the living arrangements and family size, and the controlling influence of the husband as the dominant leader of the family.

nine

✳

Conclusion

Female Kingdom Building in Mormon Fundamentalist Polygyny

I have sought to explain why women are attracted to Mormon fundamentalist society, why they remain in the polygynous group in such high numbers, and whether they fare better than men in the kingdom-building process. My findings indicate that women turn to fundamentalism to alleviate their deprivations experienced in the larger culture. I predict that the number of women in fundamentalist Mormon groups will soar because the structure accommodates deprived women from the mainsteam who are so discouraged that they are willing to share and scrounge and be formally dominated by elite polygynous men, a situation seemingly of more appeal to them than life in orthodox Mormon society.

Female Advantage in Kingdom Building

Throughout this book, I have illustrated how women are able to assimilate into the Allred culture more rapidly and easily than men do. To summarize these female advantages in kingdom building, I have used a chart, fashioned much like a board game in which men and women are the key players who move through a sequence of choices and consequence steps (figure 14). A representative conversion story further illustrates the process women go through in integrating.

The first phase of the game shows that converts experience some kind of tension—in some cases, considerable strain—prior to entering the Allred group. Only those with enduring, acute tensions eventually become Allred converts. I found that both men and women had a preexisting belief

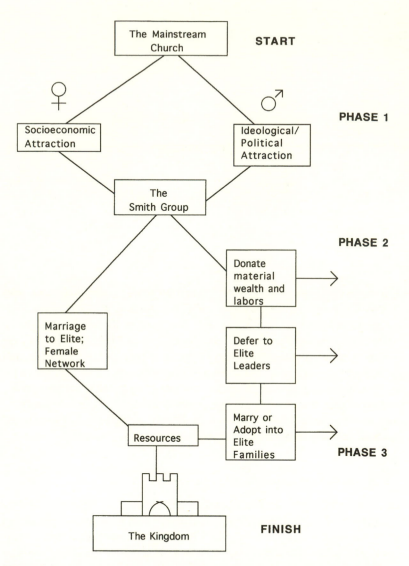

Figure 14. This flow chart represents the overall view of male and female progression in the kingdom building process. Note how women have relatively fewer obstacles in their attempts to reach the "Kingdom"—a stable, secure environment in which to raise their families and obtain autonomy. Men, however, have less direct routes to the Kindom—the acquisiton of wives and resources—and these are laden with obstacles and excessive costs.

in Mormonism, self-reliance, prophecy, eternal life (salvation), and the kingdom of God. Both sexes indicate desire for immortality and exaltation at the expense of comfortable earthlife. Both sought early Mormon ideologies to alleviate present losses. Men are drawn to the ideological prerogatives associated with higher priesthood status and the relative freedom in the pursuit of fundamentalist gospel practices and interpretations not found in the Mormon church. Women want improved socioeconomic status for themselves and their children and an escape from their marginalized placement in the orthodox Mormon church. Their motivations stem primarily from socioeconomic or marital deprivations. Their experiences in the mainstream are low economic status; single parent, divorced, widowed, or single (never married) status; exposure to Mormon ideology during childhood; and contact and interaction with parents, spouse, or other friends and family who are affiliated with the new group.

Carol

Carol is a Hispanic woman in her 40s who joined the group when she was 31.[1] She was a mainstream Mormon, employed by social services, who could not find a man in her ward or stake division who was suitable to her needs. She went through a severe depression that caused her to quit her job. She spent her days at home alone, crying and wishing that she could die. "Why had God forsaken me?" she recalls. "I was a righteous, spiritual women in my prime, and I could not progress in my righteousness without a man."

Carol reached a point in her depression when she attempted suicide and almost succeeded. She recalls that there was no special help from the people in her ward, and her family had previously disowned her for joining the Mormon church. Then, when she felt she had reached the lowest point in her life, she met a young Mormon missionary who was interested in converting to the Allred group. Carol was instantly energized by his words and began investigating the group vigorously. She found that by entering polygyny she could get married to a righteous, honorable man, who could then allow her to have children and raise them up to be "righteous seed."

Her experience in the first phase was exemplified by severe tension, depression, and a kind of cognitive dissonance between her ideals and reality. Carol was not happy in the orthodox church because she was considered unattractive or unsuitable for marriage. But in the Allred group, she realized, she could become accepted and admired. Most important, she would have the tools for progressing in the kingdom.

THE NEXT PHASE in the kingdom-building game is the acceptance of ideological tenets controlled and constructed by the male elite clergy. This phase presents many contradictory problems for convert men. While the ideal portrays the male as total sovereign over the subservient female and holding his priesthood power as leverage for her total obedience, the reality is that the woman is the sovereign over her children, her freedom, and her membership within the female network. She draws upon fundamentalist teachings to support this sovereignty. Men are actually "sovereigns" over their wives and families only once or twice a week, given their visiting schedules; all the other days, the woman is the matron of the household. The male *priesthood* also provides a mark of differentiation for women. It causes them to group themselves together out of necessity to find an alternative name, such as "motherhood," and to seek religious asylum in their own company.

Men find in this phase that they are not expected to succeed in kingdom building, at least not as a majority, whereas *all* women are expected to participate as queens and sovereigns in the heavenly kingdom.

Susan

Susan is the 50-year-old leader of the Relief Society program in the Allred group. Although she is a convert, she exerts influence and control over many established women, many of whom secretly dislike her methods but are afraid to rock the boat. Susan carries many of the mainstream programs and teachings into fundamentalism, trying to mirror her success in the mainstream onto the Allred group. Although she was not unhappy in orthodox Mormonism, she was stigmatized because of her divorce. She was the cause of her marital problems, she had been told by her bishop, and, therefore, she was to blame for the breakdown of her family.

Being strong-willed and independent, she refused to remain in a church that did "not appreciate her" and moved on to fundamentalism. Once there, she experienced a rapid rise to her position because she married well and had a strong voice. After only 2 weeks in the group, she requested the hand in marriage of a very influential councilman, the leader of a smaller order in the West Desert. Although this man was often out of town on his priesthood business, she desired to be linked with him as his wife for all eternity. The prophet approved of the marriage, and Susan settled into one of the councilman's properties, a rambler with three bedrooms near the headquarters of the group.

Susan's ascendance to her economic and political position was based primarily on her determination and her good looks. But the ease with which she rose to prestige is also dependent on the social structure. Female converts are encouraged to marry and set up autonomous households. They are further encouraged to take up new projects and be active in the community. Male converts are considered to be competitive obstacles to the community's goals, but women are assets. Thus, Susan's success is a perfect example of the second phase in kingdom building. She, like other women in the group, was accepted and promoted in the system within a relatively short time.

THE FINAL PHASE of the kingdom-building process involves a correlation between ideals and reality. To advance in kingdom building, each individual must access certain key resources and meet certain vital standards of excellence. The valued resources in the Allred group are, among other things, high social position, three or more wives in a family, economic stability and advancement, reproductive advantage, and relative independence or autonomy (being able to contribute to, but not take away from, the community's resources). These were the most common virtues preached about in Sunday meetings and informal interviews. These were the traits that were most often attached to high-status individuals and to those who claimed to be ''satisfied'' in the system.

Joan

In Joan's experience, there was a shift of values to meet her socioeconomic needs. Like many women in the orthodox Mormon church, she was stuck at home with a houseful of young children and no career skills. When her husband abandoned her and her four children, she was considering going on welfare, but her family frowned on it. ''They wanted me to find a new husband who would take care of me,'' she recalls. ''They wanted to forget that I had ever married the 'good for nothing bum' and start my life over. The problem was that I had four children by the 'bum.' What man would want me?''

Joan went to many Mormon singles dances and parties. She was still young and quite pretty. But every time she mentioned her children, the romance ended. She decided to look elsewhere. At the time she met Doug, her present husband, she was destitute and not attending church. ''I was really wild and had no desire to go back to the gospel,'' she remembers. ''And then Doug showed me a greater way to life.''

Doug promised her that she would live in relative comfort and that she would have a built-in community of friends. He said that women, not men, are the most righteous children of God and that she should just look deep inside to see the truth of it.

Over the space of 3 months, Joan attended the fundamentalist church, sitting with Doug and his wives in the third row. Her children began to play with his wives' children. She attended family gatherings and parties and felt right at home with them. At the end of the third month, she married Doug in the traditional law of Sarah ceremony. This marriage marked her conversion to the gospel and a new way of thinking about her life.

Joan's story represents the manner in which women mesh their ideals with their socioeconomic realities. Here is a woman who had rejected her belief system because her husband and family abandoned her and she became impoverished. With her membership in the new group came automatic stability and security. She embraced the new belief system, rejuvenated her own deep-seated love for the gospel, and, in the process, received economic help and female solidarity. Her new ideals of how life should be matched perfectly with her reality.

IN ANALYZING the sociopolitical and economic structures of the Allred group, I have identified several contributing factors.

1. The male-dominated religious and governmental bureaucracy provides an opposing male authority structure from which women separate themselves to form their own networks. For women to join ranks in any society, they must find commonalities, whether these commonalities are born of oppression or subjugation, or whether they are born of liberation and exultation. Commonalities may also be, simply, common interests in similar tasks and experiences.

2. Allred women unite because they do not themselves hold many powerful political or religious positions in the community (although wives of important men do greatly influence community issues). Thus, women who are dominated by their husbands build bonds with other women who are likewise officially dominated. The evidence to support this premise lies in the behavior of women when with their husbands and with other members of the male hierarchy and in their behavior when with other women. In the first case, women, giving recognition to the male authority structure, are much more constrained to behave in certain ways. In the second case, when alone with other women, a woman displays more physical and emotional freedom, without the constraint of authority or formality.

3. A great disparity exists in the distribution of resources between lower-class and elite men. The lower-class men give up or consecrate their

material assets early in the kingdom-building process, whereas elite men are already holding the assets of other converts' donations and their own industrial efforts. Female converts, although not considered to be of great wealth in this study, are more stable economically than male converts. Looked at in a business sense, there is greater turnover among male converts. Women come into the group with relatively little material wealth and opportunity for mobility and begin to establish themselves by marrying into prominent families and by engaging in network activities with established women. This activity allows them to obtain the basic material goods and services necessary to set up a simple household. Furthermore, they have more opportunity to marry up in the system and gain access to elite resources than men do. The differential access to valuable temporal resources, then, favors elite men and female converts.

These general patterns in the maintenance of gender-marked integration through the social structure indicate several key features. First, male priesthood leaders marry younger (less than half their age) women. Second, women marry up in the system and are granted releases from unwanted, lower-class husbands more readily than convert men are granted releases from unwanted wives. Third, women are arranged in independent households that, for the most part, generate their own economic provisions. Fourth, rank-and-file males are often absent for prolonged periods. Fifth, elite men more often work with their stewardships inside the community than do rogue men.[2] Thus, what I have shown in this section of my analysis of social structure is that successful integration is made up of several composite variables: political rank, marriage type, family type, networking, hypergamy, living arrangements, and years of membership. Women are simply in a much better position than men to integrate, based on access to valued resources. Women also experience fewer contradictions in meshing their ideals with their realities. Ideology states that all "God's children" should obtain the kingdom and have access to valued resources, yet nonelite men confront numerous obstacles to obtaining these resources. The ideology further states that there are more righteous women than men who are chosen to succeed in the kingdom. Men assess and test ideological "promises" or "codes" against their actual socioeconomic status and see a disparity between promises made to converts in the first two phases, conversion and commitment, and the ground rules and lack of fulfillment in the third phase, maintenance of faith. When women assess and test ideological "promises" or "codes" against their status, they see harmony between promises made to them in the first two phases and successful integration in the third phase.

In sum, the Allred polygynous system successfully constrains the flow of men, provides more marriageable, potentially reproductive women, and provides more young established dependent men than could be obtained with a more homogeneous gender system. The entire kingdom-building process is designed to promote this homogeneity and is founded on an interplay of ideology, social structure, and access to valued resources. In spite of the presence of formal subordination to male authority, the Allred group is a place where women have a significant degree of influence in the household and the community.

Implications for Future Comparative Studies of Mormon Polygyny

As industrial society declines, so does the nuclear family, and there is much experimentation and confusion as new patterns are tried. Female networking in the Allred Mormon polygynous community is one such pattern.

Many of the patterns of interrelationships I found seem to overlap with other fundamentalist groups in and around Utah (Baer 1988). Many of the same problems and conflicts found in Harker are also found among mainstream Mormon monogamists (Christenson 1972). Women in all these societies are second-class citizens who strive for influence and happiness within a constrained patriarchal framework.

Future comparative study of Mormon polygyny should aid in the explanations of two key issues: (1) marginalization, circumscription, and internal solidarity and (2) modernization and the "new" American family.

Marginalization, Circumscription, and Internal Solidarity

Because converts to the Allred group are most often the "rightwing apostates" of the Mormon church, these converts often adhere to even stricter traditional sex roles in fundamentalism. Many converts left the church because of its acceptance of "Babylonian" characteristics, such as the adoption of a shorter temple garment, the acceptance of blacks, and the changes in the temple ceremony to allow women to covenant to God rather than to their husbands. In addition, female converts leave the church because they cannot find a husband, want children, need economic shelter, or desire to live a "higher spiritual life." Both men and women in this sense are marginalized from the larger religion.

Yet, once inside the Harker branch, male converts who are not "appointees" of the council become themselves marginalized members in terms of their lack of bona fide financial stewardships and their lack of access to sanctified plural marriages; women likewise become marginalized from male patriarchal control. This marginalization is thus realized for *male converts* and for *all women* by the contradiction between the male priesthood prerogative of the formal world of financial stewardships and kingdom building, on the one hand, and heavy reliance on female economic, religious, and social contributions to family and community, on the other.

What this marginalization means to the success of female associations and to the cohesion of Harker society is that individuals who are marginalized bond with others like them, creating subcultures with the culture. George Simmel (1955), in writing about the web of group affiliations and conflict, said that women are related to any marginalized class of society, such as blue-collar workers—and, I would add, gays, blacks, migrant farm laborers, and the handicapped, among others—whose general conceptual elements have been associated with all members of society, but for some reason or other their access to the valued resources of that society is restricted. This relation is especially true for women who are removed from the formal male authority structure. In Harker, when woman are isolated from one another, they lose the ability to unite against the male structure and become slaves to the system, marginalized without internal solidarity. But when they unite in their "secondary status," they achieve the same solidarity that causes revitalization groups to join together—a sense of communion, cohesion, and united purpose.

The circumscriptive effects of Harker life on women stem from the ideological threat of losing their place in the kingdom if deviant. Threats of damnation are very common, whether these threats are self-imposed or institutionally imposed. Many women associate their marginalized status as appropriate for entrance into the celestial kingdom. They desire to live the "hardest law," in order to receive the highest rewards. For many others, these threats are imposed by the religious leaders of the community and, in some cases, by women's husbands.

It is difficult to know the actual number of women who would like to leave the community and cannot, versus those who are pleased with their lives and wish to remain. My observations, however, suggest that a significant number of women experience a variety of circumscriptive constraints based on the interview data. At least 25% women interviewed mentioned their desire to leave if they could do so without losing their children. In one interview, a woman said that her children were now members of a prominent family and that they had obligations toward that family as descendants of a powerful patriarch. When she had marital troubles and wanted to be "released" from her covenants, the patriarch of the family said that she could go but her children would remain behind to be taken care of by the other wives. A higher percentage of women interviewed indicated that they felt they must stay in order to live the "fullness," and that if they left their exaltation would be jeopardized.

Another aspect of female marginalization is the concept that women who deviate from the traditional sex roles are considered evil, with access to powerful and dangerous forces. Like the Nupe women who were accused of witchcraft by their husbands because they worked in the marketplace (Nadel 1935), Harker women also are accused of witchcraft or are scapegoated and experience a stricter marginalization in the formal political sphere because of their involvement in vital economic activities and religious ritual. In fact, it is common for women like Mary, Liz, and Vi to be labeled witches, lesbians, apostates, and devils because of their potential threat to male authority and established male-female sex roles. In sum, I found that men are counteracting egalitarian sex roles from larger society with harsher rules and restrictions for women. Ironically, this reaction only serves to reinforce solidarity and internal cohesion among women, not among men. Fear of the Gentiles' coming and stealing away children and influencing them toward evil is yet another aspect of this isolation. Members are discouraged from forming friendships outside the family and, especially, outside the community. Women's priorities in friendship are, ideally, first to her children, then to her husband, then to her sisterwife, then to her blood brothers and sisters, and then to community members. Another aspect of the circumscriptive conditions is the general ideological tenet among women that people who "go without" and suffer for a righteous cause are that much closer to the heavenly kingdom. As one woman put it, "You must live in hell to go to heaven" and be martyrs for the system. She said that there was a certain pride among women in the community in living each month on the lowest amount of money. In Harker, many wives *had* to work together to budget for their families more efficiently.

And finally, associated with the circumscriptive and marginalized conditions of women is the encouraged emigration of young men. As mentioned earlier, more young men leave the sect than young women for a variety of reasons. In a sample of young men, I found that three predominant patterns emerged to explain this emigration: lack of economic opportunities, lack of women to marry, and competition with fathers and other older men for influence and access to valued resources. One young man commented that he was threatened by a councilman to leave the branch or "face the consequences."

In sum, though women are marginalized or separated from the male political sphere and from aspects of the outside world, they are by no means passive slaves to the system. Rather, they, like other marginalized subcultures, have a degree of freedom and solidarity apart from the formal realm of society, and their actions are deemed signficant and prestigious to others in the same position.

Modernization and the "New" American Family

Of great importance in the study of Mormon polygynous interrelationships is how polygyny fits into the larger picture of the modern American family—a picture of family life that is no longer the *Leave It to Beaver* household with Ward, June, and the boys but one with a rising divorce rate, a falling marriage rate, and marginalized single mothers.

According to social anthropologist Robin Fox (1993), the breakdown of the nuclear, monogamous family is an obvious feature of our American life. I suggest that polygynous relations and other "alternative" family forms are a normal response to the change from an industrial society to a modern society, where the emphasis shifts from a situation that requires the monogamous nuclear family to one that could well accommodate a variety of extended-family patterns, including polygyny. For example, the increase in female participation in the work force and the growth of commuter employment with modern transport seems to accommodate alterations in the traditional family. The new birth technologies and the computer revolution that enables working at home further complicate family structures. A good man, in today's high-tech market, may be harder and harder to find. Many women may be more willing to share a good man than gain full use of a loser or have no man at all.

Mormon polygynous women have a profound theological support for their position that carries them through many difficulties. Other women do not. For example, in a polygynous scenario, one woman can go to work, taking the family car, and bring in adequate income for several other wives. Her co-wives could then clean the house, take care of the children, and pursue other métiers. In this scenario a husband could be able to pursue his hobbies or interests such as Alex Joseph does with his wives' financial support, or be frequently absent from home, as is the case for most Harker men. Dual-income monogamous families often must take their children to expensive, inadequate care centers and then come home to a chaotic home environment that needs cleaning and management. Certainly, the option of plural wives, plural husbands, or, for that matter, "omnigamy" (everyone married to everyone) provides a way for the modern family to survive. Certainly, monogamy seems to be in trouble in the modern, fast-paced world, and virtually no one seems to see that it was always, in fact, a "peculiar institution" to begin with.

Most plural wives are not the brainwashed prisoners pictured by the antipolygynous literature (Johanson 1990); on the contrary, in terms of economics alone, there is plenty of evidence that both in theory and practice these women work outside the home in various kinds of jobs and maintained the home and community through their *voluntary* social production activities. Furthermore, the mothers have significant control over the family. No matter how much the patriarchal order might give the husband and father top billing and how much his threat lingers in the air, it is the mother in reality who has a great deal to do with the training of their own children and the management of their households. For a man who has several wives—his rotation among them spread over great distances and periods—this point becomes even more significant. It tends, again, to place greater responsibility on the mother and serves to give her more power than she otherwise might have.

In spite of the complexity of relationships and the relative "newness" of the Mormon polygynous experiment, there is no warrant for concluding that polygyny in and of itself is an undesirable form of marriage from the point of view of stability, satisfaction of the parties, and responsibility to members. frequent divorce and remarriage, the separation of children from their parents, the multiplication of step-relationships (responsible for many child abuse cases), and the total breakdown of paternal responsibility (80% of divorced fathers at some time default on child support) all suggest that our own institution of serial monogamy is in serious trouble, not its polygynous counterpart (Fox 1993:36; Kilbride 1995). (Even though the Harker divorce rate is 35%, it is still much lower than the national rate, which is well over 50%. The fathers' default on support in Harker is not a problem—women are supported by the female network.) Furthermore, any analysis of conflict, strain, and abuse in polygynous societies should also look at the personality types associated with these conflicts and strains. Would certain types be any different in monogamous culture? Would some still be discontented, cruel, dominant, submissive, or abusive? In other words, it is my opinion that certain personality types better cope with the tides of polygyny than others and that some individuals should never go into polygyny in the first place, and this may be also true of monogamy.

It should be noted that polygyny as a marriage form is prevalent throughout the world (80% of the world's cultures practice it). In historical terms, it is monogamy that is in need of explanation, not polygamy. The Masai of Kenya, as an example of African polygyny, show attitudes and behaviors among co-wives remarkably similar to the Mormon polygynous women. Mormon women, within a worldwide context, are less peculiar to polygynous relationships.

In retrospect, and toward a clearer understanding of Mormon fundamentalist relationships and social structure, I have found that Harker women are complex individuals who form unique and sustaining relationships with other women in order to survive. The uniqueness of female relations in polygyny brings a new dimension to the dialectic of husband-wife, wife-wife family relations, requiring new theories and methods to understand and explain these relations, such as psychological anthropology, behavioral ecology, and personality analysis. The attention given to female bonding by Diane Bell (1983) supports the compelling theme of identifying female solidarity as a key to female status, satisfaction, and power. While the presence of female bonding and association may intrigue many modern feminists, the uniqueness of female ascendance in a blatantly "patriarchal" arrangement, despite the privations and difficulties, may appall many traditional feminists. The fact that it is largely the women who stay and the young men who leave is sobering. But feminist sensibilities cannot override the evidence that is presented and cases that are made here. More data and information on the processes of interrelationship *between men* must also be gathered before a final analysis can be written. Also, the complexities of convert-established family interactions should be closely evaluated to determine the exact effect differences of background have on co-wife solidarity. An in-depth study on women and men who have left the group should accompany any study of conversion and group stability. And associated with this task is the need for a deeper study of how children are affected by plural marriage and religious fundamentalism and how this system works to create secure, happy lives for some children and not for others in Mormon society.[3]

Glossary

*

Fundamentalism
Here, fundamentalism refers to the Mormon schism groups that emerged during the 1920s and 1930s after the second manifesto from the mainstream Mormon Church declaring plural marriage sinful. Although it parallels them upon many occasions, it does not necessarily duplicate the early Mormon doctrine and practices that were "fundamental" to the gospel of Joseph Smith.

Group Rather Than Cult
In this investigation, I avoid the use of the term *cult* in reference to the Allred group as it has become derogatory and misleading. I simply refer to them as a group. In short, I choose to label this group of people fundamentalist Mormons that are a sect approaching a church status. Although in Yinger's terms (1970), many schismatic groups would be cults, the Allred group is so large now that the leader is not on personal terms with every member, and they are now incorporated, as is the mainstream Mormon Church. True, the group is still at odds with the larger society in their practice of plural marriage, but they are being widely accepted and are no longer arrested for their practices.

Hypergamy
Hypergamy is the marriage of female members of a society to upper-class men, which is often associated with Indian caste systems. I use it in reference to lower-class female recruits who marry upper-class male councilmen and their appointees when they enter the group.

Integration

Here, integration refers to the longevity and staying power of participants in the Allred group. It relates to one's economic, political, and religious status in the group, and to one's gender, marriage status, and family type. It does not necessarily equate to personal happiness or contentment but, rather, refers specifically to the number of years spent in the group, the contributions one makes to the group, and the potential of staying permanmently in the group.

Keys

The keys are the sacred tools that enable men and women to unlock the mysteries of heaven, to communicate fully with God, and to regain their rightful thrones and dominions in God's kingdom. The keys are also known as the exclusive rights and privileges of the elite clergy to administer sacred ordinances among the people.

Kingdom Building (Kingdom of God)

The process of building one's earthly kingdom for the salvation and preservation of all family members and affiliates throughout the eternities. It refers specifically to one's ability to integrate well within the community and graft as many people (wives, children, appointees, adoptees) onto one's kingdom as possible. It is related to, but not necessarily dependent upon, secure finances and sound investments. Also related to kingdom building is a high male priesthood status and a correlating female support system, based on plural wife cooperation.

Polygyny

Polygyny is the marriage of one man with at least two women. It is not to be confused with the term, *polygamy,* which is the umbrella term for multiple-spouse marriage, whether husbands or wives.

The Principle

Another name for the Allred group and the commitment to the principle of plural marriage. One might hear an informant say, for example, "That man is in the Principle" or "I adhere to the Principle"; either usage is common.

Sisterwife

Sisterwife is used throughout the text to refer to a woman's co-wife. It does not necessarily relate to biological kinship, although there are nu-

merous cases of sororal and cousin polygyny, but to the religious and
economic commitment made between two women who marry the same
man, which makes them "sisters" in the gospel.

The Work

Like the Principle, the "Work" refers to the body of saints who have
committed themselves to adhering to the fullness of the gospel, including
the practice of plural marriage, the consecration of goods and talents, and
the adoption of a specific set of fundamentalist beliefs. One might hear
people say, "She is in the Work" or "I have been in the Work for four
years."

Notes

✳

Chapter 1

1. Since the Allred group is the largest polygynous group in North America, I am not cloaking their name. They are well known in historical and sociological literature, and they have participated on numerous occasions in the local Mormon "Sunstore" conferences.

2. The three theories are not always mutually exclusive. For example, the second theory allows for the "motherhood equals power" theme, whereas the first does not. The first allows for some recognition of women as separate from men, which relates to the second category that recognizes women as a group.

3. During 1992 and 1993, the hierarchy of the Mormon church began a series of "purges" of both the right and left political wings of the membership, alienating intellectuals, feminists, and gays, on the one hand, and extreme conservatives, survivalists, National Rifle Association members, and advocates of "conspiracy in government" theories, on the other (Jorgensen 1993). As a result, the Smith group has become the largest Mormon schism sect in the world and is faced with many dynamic adjustments to accommodate the large influx of rightwing Mormons.

4. During a 1993 priesthood meeting in the northern branch of the Allred group, a councilman read statistics over the pulpit to illustrate the decline of marriages in the community. He said that in 1993 there were at least three to four marriages in ten that resulted in divorce. By *divorce*, I do not mean separation but rather complete breakup of the marriage contract.

5. She has often said that she and Mary, another Harker woman, are "spiritually" trained to be able to capture a person's total character by looking in their eyes for a brief instant.

6. The total number of polygynous households in the two branches is approximately 150; thus, my sample makes up approximately 38% of the households.

Chapter 2

1. John Ray converted to the Work, in the early 1970s with ideas about socialization and psychological training that transformed much of the way people behaved in Harker. He was a pseudo-psychologist himself, with a yen for military preparedness and herbalism. He attracted huge numbers of converts to the community because of his zeal for the gospel and the commonalities he had with them. He married 12 wives and was continuing his courtship with many other young women prior to his departure from the sect in the 1980s. Although he secured a spot on the sect council of ten, he was thought of by the brethren as being too extreme in his doctrines of herbalism as a healer and his behavior with women.

2. Although Allredites claim descent through both the female and male sides of the family, they define heavenly kingdoms as being made up of patrilineal offspring, that is, offspring who trace descent through the father's side only.

3. The head god, Elohim, had spawned millions of worlds and spirits and permitted the latter bodies for occupancy of these worlds. God himself had once been a man and had advanced to godly state by this same means. This idea of eternal progression of man from mere dust to godhead appealed to both rich and poor members (Young 1954:30).

4. This commandment was extended to nonvirgins—widows, divorced, or even nondivorced believers.

5. In my analyses of political relationships in the Allred group (Bennion 1996), I argue that these dominant features of early polygyny are found in contemporary Mormon polygyny as well.

6. A further account of the Mormon Covenant Organization, vital to an understanding of the meaning attached to roles, exchanges, and status in interpersonal relationships, can be found in chapter 2 and in Cannon 1990:50–75).

7. One of the best kept secrets is the actual number of Allred group members. Like the mainstream church, Allredites keep record of and include *all* members, even if those members have left the group or are inactive. At first, I was told there are only 5,000 members, but after a colleague also conducting research on the group said that he was given the number 10,000, I spoke with many different people and at last found one who had witnessed a document containing the census of 30,000 members. I was told that he knew of members spread throughout New Mexico, Arizona, Wyoming, and other western states but that these groups were very small in number and were not considered "orders" in and of themselves. I found out later that this figure, too, was erroneous and, after reviewing one of the group's historian's records of membership, settled on the more moderate figure of 10,000.

8. It is unclear which council members have ultimate jurisdiction over which financial properties, but there is a general understanding that Priesthood Head Ben Allred has his personal trust for his family members and that his son is in managing control of the Red Cedar Corporation. The Harris brothers have jurisdiction over the Harker Construction Company, several planes, and real estate holdings such as a golf course and condominiums.

9. They have chosen their settlements to be placed among the Rockies for a purpose: According to their beliefs, it is in the Rockies that "Zion will be built."

10. Although I was told repeatedly that the prophet has sole approval over plural marriages, in reality, marriages in Harker are sanctioned and arranged, to some extent, by Brother Melvin Harris, whom I have called the "matchmaker." In theory, Melvin's brother, Matt, is the official head of Harker, but Melvin is by far the most outspoken, dominant leader of the ranch. Further, the third council member, whom I call Saul, has little power and authority in Harker, although he is the nephew of the prophet. The two dynasties—Harris and Allred—are in perpetual competition.

11. Because of the larger number of women than men in the group female labor is a significant resource (35% more women than men work in salaried positions), which would then imply that women themselves are valued in the network (Cannon 199a: 25).

12. In spite of the communal emphasis, some Harker men and women do not often go outside their own potential benefit to aid families. This pattern is normal in partial-communal societies, such as the Moshavim of Israel (Wasserfall 1993). I shall point out later, however, that women share with other women in a series of reciprocal exchanges because they must do so to survive economically.

13. Another point of dispute in the community is the question of allowing some to work hard to support others while some are collecting money on the dole. For the most part, however, members try to use the community welfare system before relying on government funds.

14. Male children of convert or nonname families are not encouraged to stay in the community.

15. Civic authority has no jurisdiction over priesthood authority in Harker. This woman, who is the city judge, cannot ultimately make judgments that are contrary to the Priesthood Council's own decisions, but she can often act as a go-between in government and priesthood matters.

16. The nuclear units of mother plus children may also constitute independent units, as in the matricentric families of British Guiana, or may be linked together, as in African polygynous societies where each co-wife and her children constitute a separate household (Smith 1956:22; Tanner 1974:37). The wealth and the nature of the husband's stewardship often determine the arrangement of co-wife residence.

17. I was later told that they get government funds for a Head Start program.

18. One family, for example, wanted to use their $20,000 insurance money to rebuild their burned home. When they opened it up for construction bid, the priesthood-owned construction company bid the highest. The company did not, however, use the $20,000 on the family's home but on a council member's home; the materials used to build the burned home were secondhand wood and materials that had already been on hand. Another woman who hurt her back in an accident was awarded an insurance claim. She wanted to buy a motorized water jet for her back, but the money was used for priesthood business instead.

19. Male networking occurs through bonds of the priesthood, through their

"brotherhood" as sons of Ephraim, and through their common experience as outcastes from the orthodox Mormon church. Because they are often "nomads" in their own families, traveling to and from wives, they find solace with other men in priesthood meeting or at a construction site where many of them work. It is here they are able to swap pleasantries about how hard it is to please their many wives, stories of *other* men's problems with wives and children, and their endless search for that lost blue sock or Sunday pair of pants. Sunday meetings also serve to strengthen the bonds of friendship and brotherhood in the gospel to which they belong.

20. Many teenage girls were married to older family men during the John Ray years, from 1975 to 1980 so these rare marriages distort the overall average age at marriage somewhat.

21. Romantic love, overall, is not a big factor in marriage unions. The first priority in securing a mate is willingness to obey the commandments of God; the second is fertility and a desire for children. Romantic love, if it happens, is co-incidental to the purpose of marriage in Harker Jankowiak and Allen 1995).

22. Though rare, an interesting element of Harker marriages can be found in the mother-daughter co-wives relationship. When a widowed or divorced woman is converted, she may bring with her an older daughter with whom she is very close. If a man is attracted to either the mother or the daughter, the other naturally requests that he marry both of them, which enable them to remain together and be provided for.

23. One common reason for the "releases," as they are called, is the lack of living space; with families who all live under the same roof, wives and children can find solace only in their overcrowded bedrooms. Other reasons given for divorce are finances, personality conflicts, and jealousies. Above all, among the women who spoke on the subject, the most common reason for a split was that "the man didn't live up to his priesthoods," either through abuse or neglect.

Chapter 3

1. Plural marriage also is the key to a new bride's status during this life and the next. Women must bear many children to keep the commandment of multiplying and replenishing the earth and to allow the waiting spirits in heaven a chance to come to earth (Young 1947).

2. Plural marriage among mainstream Mormons is generally no longer correlated with celestial marriage; rather, each male-female unit married in the temple is entered into a celestial marriage. For fundamentalists, this is generally the same doctrine; however, most individuals explained that polygyny is a prerequisite for celestial marriage.

3. Many fundamentalists claim that Jesus married Mary and Martha, the two sisters of Lazarus (Kraut 1983). God's wives are unknown, but it is believed by many Harker residents that there are several Heavenly Mothers to one Heavenly Father.

4. When I asked if Adam was a monogamist or a polygynist, one member

said that since Adam had more than one rib from which to take a wife, he had several. Further, since fundamentalists believe that Adam *is* God, Adam's wives are Eve, Lilith, and a score of other biblical women.

5. This type of "office" worship is common among mainstream Mormons as well, where all must "abide by the word of the prophet," even when the prophet is mentally and physically incapacitated.

6. Much of this information on the biblical analogies to Harker living came directly from interviews with residents of the Harker community; what I have written is their unique interpretation of the scriptures.

7. Many women use what I call "witchcraft accusations" or "scapegoating" against their husbands to gain releases from them. These accusations involve pitting their husbands against certain high-ranking leaders by claiming that they have sinned in some manner, such as "unrighteous dominion," "abuse," or "neglect." In this way, women have manipulative powers that are strategic in gaining benefits and resources.

8. Blacks, according to fundamentalists, were given the choice before being born, in the Counsel in Heaven with God, as to whether they would be willing to live the higher law and accept the responsibility the priesthood brings with it. Their reply was, no, we do not want it. Blacks, say fundamentalists, are not allowed the priesthood because they refused to accept it in an earlier life.

9. It should be noted that it is through ethnographic observation that features of female exchange are recorded and analyzed. To gain this information, I participated daily with women in their household, ecclesiastical, and outdoor activities.

10. Women raise their children within the Harker structure and use their own example as the motivational factor. They have the opportunity to raise up a rebellious seed if they so desire, but more commonly they teach obedience and respect for community leaders to their children.

11. Just as Queen Esther appeared before the king of Persia, facing death, so must all the Lord's handmaidens go when called, knowing that her sisters supported her and petitioned the lord in her behalf (Esther). Just as Mary, the mother of Jesus, and her cousin, Elizabeth, were united in their news that Mary would bear the only begotten Son of God, Harker women share news of joy of their expected child to their sisters (Matthew).

12. In one interview, a prominent wife of a councilman said the most sacred of all relationships was between two women in gospel—a relationship which, when canonized, ascended to a intimacy that enhanced the spiritual intimacy.

13. Jan is among the few woman who have received a higher privilege as wife to an apostle. Not all women have reached this heightened state of spirituality and worthiness, and they cannot perform these same priesthood rituals that she can. Further, a woman does not hold the Melchizedek Priesthood alone; she only shares this with her husband. When she marries her husband through the covenant and receives her "endowment," she then can access the priesthood but cannot bless using its name. Instead, she blesses by using Jesus Christ's name. This is the law. A woman who is in midwifery, such as Jan, finds herself in a contrary position because she may have the higher privilege, which comes only with the second

anointing, but if she uses it, she exposes this power and risks its use among women not worthy to perform it.

14. Over the years, I have heard of at least seven children who died during childbirth. Two additional cases of infant death were from internal deformities during the first year of life. Deaths such as these are rarely spoken of public, and often, in the cases of death at childbirth, the infants are quickly buried in the Harker graveyard without ceremony. No official records of births or deaths are kept.

15. Administering is giving a blessing by laying priesthood holders' hands on the head of an ill person and stating "by the power that we hold, I command you to be well." Sometimes anointing oil is used.

16. I was told by both male and female informants that council members do not condone female use of "their" powers and further suggest that women cannot perform priesthood rites without the presence of a male.

17. Again, this procedure is formally prohibited from women's use. Even for Jan, who was *worthy* to perform it, it is frowned on by Harker leaders. It became clear to me that most people do not have a clear understanding about the higher doctrines; those who do try to keep it safeguarded for fear of its misuse. There is one generation of Allred saints—whose parents were excommunicated from the church and had their endowments—who do not have the power or understanding to administer properly. Because of this 40-year gap, a number of unofficial practices pertaining to ordinances and blessings have been observed by various high and low-ranking individuals.

Chapter 4

1. As defined by Robert Carneiro (1988:61), *circumscription* refers to blockage of emigration of dissatisfied factions by features of the physical or social environment that require emigrants to suffer a decline in their standard of living. I use it here to refer to Allred women who are often barred from leaving the group through threats of damnation and the loss of their children.

2. There are patterns of ranking based on Abrahamic biblical tradition in the Harker branch of the group that closely follow lines of blood, marriage, and finance. For example, those who are more closely related to a "pure blood" or have access to valued material and priesthood resources rank higher than those who do not. Implicit in this ranking is the fact that older, established men have a higher status than younger, convert men.

3. From the hours given above, it can be figured that women, working 25 to 30 hours per week, multiplied by the 75% female workforce number of 113, contribute from 2,825 to 3,390 hours per week, while men, numbering 50, working 40 to 55 hours per week, contribute only 2,000 to 2,750 hours per week.

4. One account stated that when one woman contracted cancer, her sisterwife stayed with her night and day until she died.

5. In the larger sample of 1,808 men and women in 1993, 72% of the women

are contributing (900 women of 1,331), working on average 34 hours per week. Among the men, 83% are contributing (400 of 477). Multiply 34 hours by the 900, and the total number of hours women contribute are on average 30,600 collective hours per week, while the men who contribute, numbering 400, working on average 45 hours per week, provide only 18,000 hours per week.

6. In most polygynous communities outside Mormonism, only the richest men of the village are able to have plural wives. Here men with or without substantial capital are able to accumulate wives, so that the wives have to often fend for themselves.

7. In interviewed Judith's husband and many like him who have several wives and work in some sort of manual occupation. I found him to be a sincere, hardworking man who realized that his meager income could not be split effectively four ways and was resigned to leave it to his wives to manage how they could. "It is part of their duty as plural wives to be responsible for their own stewardships—their own sovereignties."

Chapter 5

1. I was told of more incidents of young men who left the group than young women, and when I recorded the number of young adults aged 18 to 24, the females far outnumbered the males.

2. The Harker Council reserves the right to allow certain families birth control devices.

3. Harker has one of the largest number of honor roll students, athletes, and student officers in the district.

4. It is common for women who have been divorced or widowed while in the orthodox Mormon church to be converted to fundamentalism.

5. One young man told me he was known as the "stinky goat boy" of Harker because he came from a lower-class family. But he gleamed with pride in qualifying this statement: "At least I'm not a Witlock—boy, they're are the lowest of them all."

6. Harker conducted a "bad boy roundup," gathering approximately eight boys who were accused of stealing tithing and breaking into the Harker mercantile. The boys were put in a dark potato cellar for a week without plumbing or running water as punishment for this crime. Several informants noted physical punishments like "getting whipped with a hose" or "smacking them with a two by four."

7. The sacrament is a ritual not unlike the Protestant Communion, in which bread and wine (in this case water) are eaten by the congregation in representation of the body and blood of Christ. In Harker, as well as in the Mormon church, this ritual is a renewal of the covenants they make to Christ.

8. There is an entire separate language used to describe the activities surrounding a "testimony." Because this testimony is an inner assurance of a person's belief and devotion to the structure, it is highly encouraged and promoted within the community. As a child, one gradually "builds" one's testimony. As

an adult, one "strengthens" one's testimony. During Sacrament Meeting, all "bear" their testimonies, which is to stand and speak of one's faith to all present in the room, as with the orthodox Mormon church.

9. In a small survey of young women in several youth religious meetings I attended, I noted that not one girl said anything bad about polygynous lifestyle. Most talked about their courtship experiences and how much they looked forward to being mothers. These were educated, popular girls. One girl, however, said she was going to wait until she was at least 22, so that she could finish her college degree.

10. Men, both married and single, of *any* age may marry. For this reason, I have indicated a male age range of "20 to 80." It is not uncommon for an elderly man to take a young wife, though this type of marriage is more common in the Colorado City, Arizona, fundamentalist branch than in Harker.

11. Patriarchal blessings are given to orthodox Mormon youths as well, although they are not required. Within the Mormon church and within Harker, blessings are given by a priesthood holder who has been set apart as patriarch, which is a life calling.

12. One common reason for divorce is lack of living space, where in families who all live under the same roof, wives and children can find solace only in their overcrowded bedrooms. Other reasons given for divorce include finances, personality conflicts, and jealousies. Above all, among the women who spoke on the subject, the most common reason for a split was that "the man didn't live up to his priesthoods," either through abuse or neglect.

13. As to the sealing itself, the procedure for plural wives is the same for first marriages. The particpants are clothed in their official undergarment, over which is worn a loose white cotton or linen robe. The bride and groom kneel before a simple altar or in front of the administrator of the ceremony. The couple clasp hands in a sacred manner over the altar, and they covenant to keep God's commandments and to be faithful to each other. If, in the case of plural marriages, the ceremony is far from home or the first wife has not given consent, other wives may not accompany the couple.

14. Though it is more usual to have more than one witness at the wedding, the obscurity of the "hidden room" is common in plural marriage ceremonies. Because bigamy is a third-degree felony offense in their state and men may lose their jobs if they are found out to be polygynists, marriages are kept extremely quiet, with only a few family members, other wives, and the priesthood authority who conducts the ceremony present.

15. It was called "lookout" because it was used as a spy tower during the "golden years" of John Ray, when couples would rotate guard duty and make notes of anybody coming and going from Harker. It was often used as a "make-out" spot for couples.

16. In *Doctrine & Covenants* 76:53, this promise is somewhat explained: "and who overcome by faith, and are sealed by the Holy spirit of promise, which the Father sheds forth upon all those who are just and true." For Harker residents,

this promise is a fulfillment that their office will be sanctioned from God and that they will be blessed in their marriage.

17. One woman said she had wanted to be blessed with the garment for years but was denied entrance into the endowment house because her husband was not true to his priesthoods. So, both the man and the woman must be worthy to obtain garments. It is considered a great privilege.

18. Sally gave me an analogy of a circle of blue marbles to illustrate her "outcast" status in her marriage. She said she stands outside the circle of marbles, wanting desperately to have the blue ones. But her husband was giving the precious blue marbles to some other woman; though she pleaded with him to share, he only gave her the clear or whitish ones.

19. It is common for pure blood (established) families to practice the levirate form of marriage. I heard of at least four of these marriages in the last 6 years. In this way, pure blood families can keep the children of the dead husband in the family and further keep any additional progeny by his brother in the same kingdom.

20. This story is a compilation of several women's lives and not a description of any single woman's experience. It is representative of the kinds of activities that occurred during the John Ray years, when obedience to the husband's rule at all costs was of utmost importance.

21. This story is an excerpt from a longer interview conducted indirectly through a friend of the informant. This friend is responsible for the compilation and "telling" of the story and should receive acknowledgment for it.

22. I was told varying interpretations of this story. One member said that Tina's husband was accused of being an adulterer and left the Allred group. His other wives were then assimilated into other families. Another said that this man is still in the group but is no longer cruel in his treatment of his wives. Whichever is the case, I have intentionally cloaked this story with events and facts from other women's lives so that no one woman or man will ever be identified.

Chapter 6

1. It is common for a middle-aged woman to have babies at the same time as her oldest daughters. From 40 to 50, Harker women are still building their families, having already had six or seven children.

Chapter 7

1. "Heavenly quota" refers to the number of children either a man and woman have discussed having or what a woman sees visions of having. As noted, women often have "feelings" or "visions" about certain children who are waiting in heaven to come down specifically to her family.

2. Ann was often told, after joining the group, that she would be able to bear

children when she got "enough faith." They said they were praying for her to do so.

Chapter 8

1. One could argue that *all* women engage in these same activities—that is, all women who are economically disadvantaged and must do so for survival. I suggest that many factors—the recessed Bitterroot Valley, the absence of males, the pseudo-communal atmosphere, the emphasis on Gentile (larger society) corruption—all lend to the argument that these activities are prototypical of Harker women.

2. See the section on economic contribution in chapter 4 or Singh and Morey's study (1987) of the value of work at home and contribution of wives' household service in polygynous families.

3. In Kenya, even numbers of wives are preferred to avoid "odd woman out."

Chapter 9

1. Although the Allred group frowns on dark-skinned peoples they convert many Hispanics. Hispanics are considered to be "Lamánites," Indians, grafted members of the House of Judah.

2. Rogue males are lower-class, rank-and-file males who much like rogue or non-alpha chimpanzees, are unable to access valued resources and females.

3. Phil Kilbride, a social anthropologist, has written a book on polygyny in America (1995) that explores alternative forms of family living in modern society. He believes that plural marriage as an option, at least in theory, may be better than a high rate of divorce and remarriage on the emotional lives of children now at risk to divorce in America.

References

✳

Aberle, David. 1972. "A Note on Relative Deprivation Theory as Applied to Millenarian and Other Cult Movements." In *Reader in Comparative Religion*, 3rd ed. William Lessa and Evon Vogt, eds., pp. 203–214. New York: Harper and Row.

Acker, Joan, et al. 1981. "Feminism, Female Friends, and the Reconstruction of Intimacy." *Research in the Interweave of Social Roles: Friendship*, 2:75–108.

Allred, Vance. 1984. "Mormon Polygamy and the Manifesto of 1890—A Study of Hegemony and Social Conflict." Thesis for master's degree, Missoula: University of Montana.

Altman, I., and J. Ginat. 1996. *Polygamous Families in Contemporary Society.* Cambridge: Cambridge University Press.

Arrington, Leonard J. 1955. "The Economic Role of Pioneer Mormon Women." *Western Humanities Review* 9:145–64.

———. 1971. "Blessed Damozels: Women in Mormon History." *Dialogue* 6 (2): 22.

Baer, Hans. 1976. "The Levites of Utah: The Development of and Recruitment to a Small Millenarian Sect." Ph.D. dissertation, Salt Lake City: University of Utah.

———. 1988. *Recreating Utopia in Desert.* New York: SUNY Press.

Barnes, J. A. 1954. "Class and Committee in a Norwegian Island Parish." *Human Relations* 7:39.

Bateson, Mary Catherine. 1989. *Composing a Life.* New York: Atlantic Monthly Press.

Bauer, Janet. 1993. Discussant address for the invited session, "Gender and Religious Fundamentalism Cross-Culturally." American Anthropological Association meetings, Washington, D.C.

Bean, Lee. 1990. *Fertility Change on the American Frontier.* Berkeley University of California Press.

Bell, Diane. 1983. *Daughters of the Dreaming.* Melbourne: McPhee Gribble/Allen and Unwin.

Bennion, Janet. 1996. "Kings, Queens, and Covenants: An Analysis of Male and Female Conversion and Integration in a Mormon Polygynous Community." Ph.D. dissertation, Salt Lake City: University of Utah.

Bradley, Martha S. 1990. "The Women of Fundamentalism: Short Creek, 1953." *Dialogue* 23(2):15–37.

Brink, Judy. 1993. "Lost Rituals: Rural Sunni Women in Egypt." Paper delivered at American Anthropological Association meetings, Washington, D.C.

Bronson, Lorraine. 1982. *Winnie* (in-house Harker literature not in print).

Bruce, Steve. 1990. Modernity and Fundamentalism: The New Christian Right in America. *BJS* 41(4):478–95.

Cannon, Janet. 1992. "Of One Flesh. Family Living Arrangement Strategies in a Contemporary Mormon Polygynist Commune Society for the Scientific Study of Religion conference paper," Washington, D.C. Nov.

Cannon, Janet (name changed later to Bennion). 1990. "An Exploratory Study of Female Networking in a Mormon Fundamentalist Society." Thesis for master's degree, Portland, Oregon: Portland State University.

Carneiro, Robert. 1980. The Circumscription Theory: Challenge and Response." American *Behavioral Scientist* 31:497–511.

Christ, Carol P. 1980. *Diving Deep and Surfacing: Women Writers on Spiritual Quest.* Boston: Beacon Press.

Christensen, Harold. 1972. *Dialogue: A Journal of Mormon Thought* 7(4): 20

Cooper, Rex. 1990. *Promises Made to the Fathers.* Salt Lake City: University of Utah Press.

Driggs, Ken. 1990. "Twentieth Century Polygamy and Fundamentalist Mormons in Southern Utah," 3 January, Cedar City, Utah: Dixie College Performing Arts Symposium.

Eiesland, Nancy. 1993. "Adult Female Converts to Classical Pentecostalism." Paper presented at the American Anthropological Association meeting in Washington, D.C.

Embry, Jessie. 1987. *Mormon Polygamous Families: Life in the Principle.* Salt Lake City, Utah: University of Utah Press.

Evans, Sarah. 1989. *Born for Liberty: A History of Women in America.* New York: Free Press.

Foster, Lawrence. 1984. *Religion and Sexuality: The Shakers, the Mormons, and the Oneida Community.* University of Illinois Press: Urbana and Chicago.

Fox, Robin. 1993. *Kinship and Marriage.* Cambridge: Cambridge University Press.

Fox, Robin. 1993. *Reproduction and Succession: Studies in Anthropology, Law, and Society.* New Brunswick, N.J.: Transaction Publishers.

Friedl, Erika. 1989. *Women of Deh Koh.* Washington, D.C.: Smithsonian Institution Press.

————. 1993. "Ideal Womanhood in Postrevolutionary Iran." Paper delivered at American Anthropological Association meeting, Washington, D.C.

Geertz, Clifford. 1972. "Deep Play: Notes on the Balinese Cockfight." *Daedalus* 101:1–37.

Glock, Charles. 1973. "On the Origin and Evolution of Religious Groups." In *Religion in Sociological Perspective: Essays in the Empirical Study of Religion*, Charles Y. Glock and Belmont, eds. Calif.: Wadsworth.

Gluckman, Max. 1963. "Gossip and Scandal." *Current Anthropology* 4:307–16.

Goodson, Stephanie S. 1976. "Plural Wives" In *Mormon Sisters*, Claudia Bushman, ed. Salt Lake City: Olympus Publishing.

Hanks, Maxine. 1992. *Women and Authority: Re-emerging Mormon Feminism.* Salt Lake City: Signature Books.

Jackson, Michael. 1982. *Allegories of the Wilderness*. Bloomington: Indiana University Press.

Jankowiak, W., and E. Allen. 1995. "The Balance of Duty and Desire in an American Polygamous Community." In *Romantic Passion*. New York: Columbia University Press.

Johanson, Pat. 1990. "Twelve Reasons Why Not to Marry a Polygynist," personal writings. Unpublished paper distributed by Johnson in Salt Lake City.

Jones, Blurton. 1987. "Tolerated Theft, Suggestions about the Ecology and Evolution of Sharing, Hoarding and Scrounging." *Social Science Information* 26:31.

Jorgensen, Chris. 1992. "It's Judgment Day for Far Right: LDS Church Purges Survivalists." *Salt Lake Tribune*, November 29, pp. A1.

———. 1995. *Plural Marriage for Out Times: A Reinvented Option?* Westport, CT: Bergin and Garvey Press.

Kilbride, Phillip. 1990 *Encounters with American Ethnic Cultures*, University of Alabama Press.

Kraut, Ogden. 1983. *Polygamy in the Bible*, Salt Lake City: Pioneer Press.

———. 1989. "The Fundamentalist Mormon." Speech presented at the *Sunstone* Symposium, August.

Langness, L. L. 1987. *The Study of Culture*, Navato, CA: rev. ed. Chandler & Sharp Publishers.

Leacock, Eleanor. 1978. "Woman's Status in Egalitarian Society: Implication for Social Evolution." *Current Anthropology* 19:247.

Lofland, John. 1977. *Doomsday Cult*. New York: Irvington Press.

Logue, Larry. 1984. "Time of Marriage: Monogamy and Polygamy in a Utah Town." *Journal of Mormon History* 4:3–26

Murphy, Yolanda, and Robert F. Murphy. 1985. *Women of the Forest*. New York: Columbia University Press.

Musisi, Nakanike. 1991. "Women Elite Polygyny and Buganda State Formation." *Signs* 16(41):757–77.

Musser, Joseph W. 1944. "Celestial or Plural Marriage." *Truth*, pp. 102

———. 1948. "The Inalienable Rights of Women." *Truth*, pp. 134.

Nadel, S. 1935. "Nupe State and Community." *Africa* 8:257.

Parker, Seymour, Janet Smith, and Joseph Girat. 1975. "Father Absence and Cross-Sex Identity: The Puberty Rites Controversy Revisted." *American Ethologist* 2:687–705.

Powell, J. 1871 [quoted in] Isn't One Wife Enough? by Kimball Young. New York: Holt and Company.

Pratt, Orson, 1874. Rules of Conduct. *The Seer*, London: F. D. Richards Press.

Quinn, Michael D. 1985. "LDS Church Authority and New Plural Marriages, 1890–1904." *Dialogue* 18 (Spring): 9–105.

Sacks, Karen. 1974. *Engels Revisited:Women, the Organization of Production, and Private Property: Toward an Anthropology of Women*. New York and London: Monthly Review Press.

Scott, Ruth. 1989. "Record of Harker History" (informant recorded statement, not in print).

Sered, Susan. 1994. *Priestess, Mother, Sacred Sister: Religious Dominated by Women*. New York: Oxford University Press.

Simmel, Georg. 1955. *Conflict and the Web of Group Affiliations*. Chicago: The Free Press.

Sinclair, Karen. 1986. "Women and Religion." In *The Cross-Cultural Study of Women*, Margot Duley and Mary Edwards, eds. New York: Feminist Press.

Singer, Merrill. 1978. Unpublished field notes on Mormon polygyny.

Singh, Ram D., and Mathew J. Morey. 1987. "The Value of Work-at-Home and Contributions of Wives' Household Service Polygynous Families: Evidence from and African LDC." *Journal of Economic Development and Cultural Change*, 141–160.

Smith, Raymond T. 1956. *The Negro Family in British Guiana*. London: Routledge and Paul Press.

Solomon, Dorothy A. 1984. *In My Father's House*. New York: Franklin Watts.

Tanner, Nancy. 1974. "Matrifocality." *Women, Culture and Society*, M. Z. Rosaldo and L. Lamphere, eds. Stanford Calif.: Stanford University Press.

Taylor, Samuel W. 1956. *I Have Six Wives: A True Story of Present-day Plural Marriage*. New York: Greenburg.

Tullidge, Edward. 1877. *Women of Mormonism*. New York: Tullidge and Crandall.

Van Wagoner, R. S. 1986. *Mormon Polygamy: A History*. Salt Lake City: Signature Books.

Wagner, Jan. 1982. *Sex Roles in Contemporary American Communes*. Bloomington: Indiana University Press.

Warenski, Marilyn. 1980. *Patriarchs and Politics: The Plight of the Mormon Woman*. New York: McGraw-Hill.

Wasserfall, R. 1993. "Continuity and Struggle: Two Generations of Jewish Moroccan Men in a Moshav in Israel." Paper delivered at the 1993 American Anthropological Association meeting, Washington, D.C.

Watson, Marianne. 1986–1993. Notes and observations by the Harker group historian.

Weber, Max. 1930. *The Protestant Ethic and the Spirit of Capitalism*. London: Allen & Unwin.

Wheeldon, P. H. 1969. "Norms and Manipulations of Relationships in a Work Context." In *Social Networks in Urban Situations*, J. Mitchell, ed. Manchester: Manchester University Press.

Widstoe, John. 1939. *Discourse of Brigham Young.* Salt Lake City: Desert Book Company.

Wright, Lyle. 1963. "Origins and Development of the Church of the First-Born of the Fullness of Time." Thesis for mastu's degree, Salt Lake City: Brigham Young University.

Yinger, Milton. 1970. *The Scientific Study of Religion.* New York: Macmillan.

Young, Brigham. 1861. "Divorce and Marriage Law of the Celestial Kingdom." Discourse in Salt Lake Tabernacle, reported by George Watt, Church Archives.

Young, Kimball. 1947. "Sex Roles in Polygynous Mormon Families." *Readings in Psychology,* Theodore Newcomb and Eugene Hartley, eds. New York: Holt.

——. 1954. *Isn't One Wife Enough?* New York: Holt.

Mormon Literature

The following is a list of Mormon scripture and literature that is not listed in the references.

Journal of Discourses. 26 vols. Liverpool: Latter-Day Saints' Book Depot, 1854–86. A compilation of speeches by prominent nineteenth-century LDS leaders.

LDS Archives. Library and Archives, Historical Dept., Church of Jesus Christ of Latter-Day Saints, Salt Lake City, Utah.

"Moses," from the *Pearl of Great Price.* 1981. Salt Lake City, Utah: Church of Jesus Christ of Latter-day Saints

"Alma" and "Mosiah," from the *Book of Mormon.* 1981. Salt Lake City, Utah: Church of Jesus Christ of Latter-day Saints

Isaiah, Proverbs, Psalms, Deuteronomy, Genesis, Timothy, Peter, Ephesians, Luke, John, Matthew, and *Corinthians,* from the King James Version of the Bible, as translated by Joseph Smith.

Doctrine & Covenants, a volume of Mormon scripture containing letters, directives, and selections from the revelations given to Joseph Smith.

Relief Society Study Guide and *Priesthood Guide.* 1988–1989. Published by the LDS Church, Salt Lake City, a study guide for LDS men and women.

History of the Church of Jesus Christ of Latter-Day Saints. 1978. 6 vols. Introduction and notes by B. H. Roberts. Salt Lake City: Deseret Book.

Index

✳